You Got This!

Practical Training for Purposeful Living

Fritz T. Moga, editor

I Street Books
Lincoln, California

Library of Congress Cataloging-in-Publication Data

Moga, Fritz T.
YOU GOT THIS! Practical Lessons for Purposeful Living
ISBN-13: 978-1099371233

1. Christian Life 2. Health & Fitness 3. Personal Growth

Printed in the United States of America.

Cover Design by K.D. Dehnert

I Street Books
A simple place, restful and peaceful, where all thoughts are valued and all people welcomed.

DEDICATION

This book is dedicated to the men and women across the globe who have had anything to do with our university. This includes staff and faculty who have worked tirelessly to bring quality education and life-change to our students. Countless are proud alumni and some are still students today. It's been my honor to have known so many of you over the years that I've been associated with San Jose Bible College / San Jose Christian College / William Jessup University!

To that end, all proceeds from this book will go towards student scholarships to help educate and empower the next generation of world changers.

TABLE OF CONTENTS

Foreword   *Dr. David Timms*

Preface

Introduction   1

Chapter 1   Who Am I?   7
                 Finding Identity in Christ
                 Matthew Godshall

Chapter 2   Spiritual Muscles   15
                 Developing a Disciplined Rhythm
                 Mark Moore

Chapter 3   Upwards   23
                 Overcoming Through God's Word
                 Derek Zahnd

Chapter 4   Turn Down the Volume   29
                 Restoring Quiet Times
                 Ryan Murphy

Chapter 5   I Can Relate   37
                 Discovering Sacred Pathways
                 Kay Llovio

Chapter 6   Don't Worry – Be Happy   45
                 Learning to Seek First the Kingdom
                 Fritz Moga

Chapter 7   Downtime is Not Wasted Time   53
                 Taking Time to Rest
                 Libby Backfish

Chapter 8	Walk, Bike, Hike, Breathe	59
	The Importance of Movement	
	Parker Daniells	

Chapter 9	Tree Forts & Piles of Snow	67
	How Being in Nature is a Game Changer	
	Fritz Moga	

Chapter 10	You Are What You Eat	73
	Creating a Nutritious Diet	
	Laura Hall	

Chapter 11	Creativity is Not a Luxury	81
	Exploring the Arts	
	Emily Hill	

Chapter 12	Into the Deep End	89
	Drowning in Technology & Social Media	
	Matt Bach	

Chapter 13	No Time!	97
	Practical Time Management	
	Michael Obermire	

Chapter 14	Moving Forward	105
	Successful Goal Setting	
	Michael Obermire	

Chapter 15	The Power of Saying "No"	113
	Making Yes a Matter of Priority	
	Dave Heitman	

Chapter 16	Boats & Best Intentions	119
	Career and Life Planning	
	Christy Jewell	

Chapter 17   Better Bank Accounts   127
               Healthy Financial Habits
               Steve Backers

Chapter 18   Stormy Weather Ahead   135
               Are You Prepared?
               Kristen Crichton

Chapter 19   Stress   143
               Our Close Friend...What?
               Melanie Trowbridge

Chapter 20   The Giants of Anxiety & Depression 151
               When Stress is NOT Our Friend
               Melanie Trowbridge

Chapter 21   When Just a Friend Won't Do   159
               It's Time for the Big C!
               Meghan McMahon Johnson

Chapter 22   Any Second Now   167
               Persevering Through Problems
               Thomas Fitzpatrick

Chapter 23   Don't Get Burned – Out   175
               Beating Busyness & Burnout
               Fritz Moga

Chapter 24   Becoming a (Self) Care-Giver 183
               Avoiding the Toxicity of Life
               Erin Ambrose

Chapter 25   I'll Be There For You   191
               Nurturing Solid Friendships
               Mandy Schmidt

Chapter 26   From Isolation to Community   199
Discovering Strength in Others
Daniel Gluck

Chapter 27   Sharing the Journey   207
Finding or Being a Mentor
Fritz Moga

Chapter 28   Get Over Yourself   215
The Blessing of Serving Others
Mary Ann McMillan

Chapter 29   Surprised by Joy   223
Delighting in Life
Erin Hill

Chapter 30   An Attitude of Gratitude   229
The Impact of Practicing Thankfulness
Dawn Pickering

Chapter 31   Lighten Up!   235
Learning to Laugh & Play More
Fritz Moga

Contributing Authors' Bios   243

Endnotes   253

Foreword

Many cultures have formal and informal ways to pass down the wisdom of the elders to following generations. Tribal elders might gather around campfires or in community longhouses. Parents and grandparents might use rites of passage as an opportunity to speak into the lives of younger members of the community.

We generally have none of these mechanisms. With the steady demise of the family unit, the high level of mobility (especially from rural to urban settings), and the value placed on individualism, we seldom listen well to each other. It has come at great cost.

One of the few sustained rites of passage in our culture is the undergraduate college experience. Yes, on average, people with undergraduate degrees will earn $1 million more over a lifetime than people without an undergraduate degree. Yes, a liberal arts education prepares young adults to think critically and deeply; to innovate and problem-solve. But the undergraduate experience is about something else, too.

An increasingly common term I hear these days is "adulting." It's the process of young people transitioning from being high school students to responsible and capable adults in society. This has become a key (if a little surprising) value of the college experience. College and university is not just about traditional education but also about important transitions. On the one hand, students are learning skills and expertise in particular fields of academic endeavor. On the other hand, they are also learning how to live.

Many students arrive at University without any cooking experience, barely able to operate a washing machine, and far from ready to manage their own finances responsibly. Some of those students will leave four years later without having made much progress in these basic life skills. We don't offer classes on effective laundering (clothes, not money), food preparation, debt management, or social skills. We don't have a lot to say about time management, stress management, or meaningful recreation. Perhaps we should. Everyone assumes these things can be caught, since they are not taught. And the basic wisdom of the ages (on these and a myriad of other life topics) often falls by the wayside.

That's why I'm delighted that my friend and colleague Fritz Moga has had a vision for this book. He has gathered "the elders" together and asked them to speak (okay, write) to the generations that are following behind and anyone else who wants to continue to grow in life. He has also written some pretty insightful chapters himself.

The old adage declares that "it takes a village to raise a child." Those of us who are parents know how very true that is. We depend on mentors, friends, and other people to speak into the lives of our children. As a father of three sons myself, I know that if I say something it may bounce right off them, but if a family friend (or someone they respect) says the same thing it can pierce between bone and marrow. We truly need each other. That's how God works. He works within us as he works between us.

That's what makes this book so significant. It captures life-wisdom from so many people; people who live and work with young adults every day; people who understand the fears and needs in this transitional season of life; people who have a heart to strengthen this "rite of passage" that we call college.

Of course, this book serves not just college students but *all of us*. Wisdom doesn't have an expiration date or any kind of exclusive application. We could all benefit from this book because it is about life — all of it.

Welcome to this campfire and these words of life. I've read every chapter and I commend it to you. I'm confident that if you will hear and heed these words, you will live well!

David Timms
Dean, School of Christian Leadership
William Jessup University
July 2019

Preface

I love what I do! It is a blessing to teach and prepare college students to go out and work with teenagers, helping make a difference in their lives. I started working with teenagers myself as a volunteer with Young Life when I was fresh out of high school. It was there I had my first opportunities to teach the Word of God, go to camps, and begin to hear the life stories of teenagers.

My first career was as the athletic director at a Christian junior high school. I continued teaching (P.E. and science) but also led the chapel program. My favorite experiences were the road trips I would take with my athletes going to compete at other schools. It was in those cramped seats of a big yellow bus that students' stories would begin to pour out. Hurt, frustration, broken families, academic pressures and issues of identity led the list of conversations on the bus.

Those early experiences led me full-time into youth ministry. I worked at two churches running programs for junior high, high school and occasionally college students. Weekly meetings, more road trips to camps and conferences and missions trip continued to allow me time to teach and work with students. And the conversations about life continued.

After almost 19 years of vocational youth ministry, I came to a Christian college where everything I had done before was expanded. There were differences between church and the ministry at the college. First, I was now able to see and interact with my students every day of the week unlike one or two days at church. Second, the issues college students were dealing with were much more intense than those of my former students in high school.

I continue to teach classes but I've always considered myself as a pastor who teaches, not the other way around. The relationships I have with students drive me to teach well but also to make sure I am taking time to get to know them. There are still road trips and missions experiences where we may be together 24/7 for up to three weeks! Imagine the conversations that can happen over that amount of time.

My first day on the job almost 20 year ago I told the faculty and staff at then San Jose Christian College (now William Jessup University) that I hoped they liked me because I had no plans on leaving…with God's blessing, I still don't!

I'm thankful to God who has allowed me the privilege of working with teenagers and college students for the last 30 years. I've been blessed to walk alongside them and learn from them as well. It has been a life well lived.

I work in an amazing environment at William Jessup University as part of the Faculty of Theology and the School of Leadership. My co-workers, many whom have contributed to this book, are a group of godly women and men who love teaching the Word of God but also know how to enjoy life as they do this. Thanks to our Dean, Dr.

David Timms, who allows us opportunities for creative growth and empowers us to take risks and go for it!

A big shout out to all my students from the last 19 years for allowing me to barge into their lives as a professor and friend. The following list comprises my spring 2019 students who contributed lists and took surveys to come up with the chapter ideas, potential authors and the name of the book: Abby Armienta, Dan Adams, Micaiah Lum, Jenna Ramirez-Kirgan, Landon Shaffer, Aubrey Muffett, Megan Johnson, Mia Gliatta, Scott McIntosh, Caleb Gonsalves, Grant Sork, Conrad Carroll, Maddy Harvey, Jakan Hoag, Clayton Holmes, Ian Jeffries, Christie Kovaly, Kodiak Miller, Makenna Shrum, Kaylee Surrel, Ashlyn Carey, Wyatt Cooper, Jesse Herzer, AJ Mendoza, Cassidy Gray, Nallely Velasco, Katie Camerer, Harpreet Chumber, Brenna Campbell, Sophia Sidle, Nathan Cortez, Tyler Barton, Jessica Peterson, Debra Hay, Matthew Meek, Britteny Dunn, Bradley Baum, Meagan Charlton, Eric Hayes, Cassie Hinton, Katelin Unversaw, Amanda Holtzen, Malie Jackson, Nick Tucker, Ethan Stout, Mikey Koons, Tayler Gibbs, Candice Henthorn, and Ryan Humphrey.

Lastly, I want to thank the 25 authors who decided to take this journey with me. I asked and they answered. Each person took time, thought and energy to produce great chapters. Thanks for your patience as I learned to edit by sending our chapters back and forth. I appreciate each one of you. You have put together a great book.

Fritz Moga, May 19, 2019

Introduction

At the end of an exercise class on one occasion, I overheard two women talking next to me. The subject was anxiety. This didn't surprise me as it seems anxiety is running rampant these days. What did surprise me was they were not talking about themselves being stressed but about their children! The two women shared about the fast pace of life, the overwhelming expectations placed on their children and the fact that so much information (through technology) comes at them so quickly. One mom said her "cure" was to make sure at every dinner to go around and say what they were each thankful for that day; seeing gratefulness as the antidote for anxiety.

I actually jumped into the conversation at this point, something I'm not a stranger to doing, and asked the age of their children. Both had just girls, one woman's daughter was just over four years old, the other woman had two daughters, eight and eleven years old. Four, eight and eleven! How dare we be talking about anxiety and stress in children that young! But then again how dare we not, right?

Just over 25 percent of children ages 13-18 suffer from anxiety disorders. These young people tend to worry about things such as grades, peer relationships, sports performances and family issues.[1] Research shows that "untreated children with anxiety disorders are at higher risk to perform poorly in school, miss out on important social experiences, and engage in substance abuse".[2]

Of course worry and anxiety did not first develop in children! Generalized Anxiety Disorder (GAD) affects 6.8 million adults, or 3.1% of the U.S. population. Women are twice as likely to be affected as men (most likely because they have to co-exist with men).[3]

WHY THIS BOOK? WHY NOW?

I have spent a majority of my life working with teenagers and young adults in both vocational church ministry as well as teaching at a university. The idea for this book comes out of those experiences, watching our young adults go from bad to worse – from marginal anxiety behaviors to such an increased level that they end up in bed not able to get up, get out, or function on a daily basis. Here's how a few of my current students expressed anxiety in their lives:

> *"Anxiety has been a part of my life for as long as I can remember. Rapid heartbeat and nervous jitters of pain have been my companions on many a night. This in a lot of ways has gotten worse as I have started college. So much is expected of me from so many different places, and the pressure to be perfect is often around me. So I strive to achieve a level at which I was never meant to operate, which ultimately causes my anxiety to repeat and worsen. This is a cycle I am all too familiar with."* Caleb.

> *"I'm mostly an introvert, but there are certain times and with certain people where I can be extroverted. I also have anxiety and a lot of times it's worse than just being nervous, it's the kind where I have to force myself to leave my dorm for class or a meal or even to hang out with friends. These are pretty big challenges as a college student*

and someone who doesn't want to isolate herself, but also doesn't want to feel overwhelmed by people. I have to make myself do things that are uncomfortable for myself or I'll get stuck in a rut that I can't get out of. My anxiety turns into depression pretty easily if I don't make myself get out of the bubble I create for myself." Candice

"The American society asks so much of young people and completely undermines those who cannot keep up. If you're not in AP classes, if you don't have a job, if you're not successful in a sport and you didn't know the right people and if you don't have some magnificent obtainable plan for your future then you're thrown to the side. This is what I experienced while in high school and although I thought I was able to keep up and keep it together when I got to college it all caught up to me." Maddy

"I am an over-achieving, high-stress-thriving perfectionist with the talent to back it up. On the outside I look like a parent or a pastor's dream kid. But in reality, there is a heavy load of expectations tied up with A-plus grades and shining performances. If I am honest with myself, I know that the expectations placed on me by family, teachers, pastors, bosses, God (just being honest here) and mainly myself can quickly turn a joy-filled life of effective ministry into a constant effort to maintain perfection. It's exhausting. I cycle through seasons of excellent work only to end up in an overwhelmed blob on the floor. But what is the alternative to striving? Slack off? Waste my time and talent? That doesn't sound any better. I'd rather work myself beyond capacity than disappoint." Makenna

What about you? Would you potentially use any of the following words or phrases to describe you or your life right now: overworked, anxious, burdened, stressed, under pressure, high expectations, work stress, family life issues, poor health, the future, current financial situation?

Perhaps that list doesn't describe you so much but instead those around you; friends, a spouse, children, and co-workers. If so this book is for you.

THE HOPE

This book isn't specifically about anxiety nor just about college students but about how the pressures, concerns and unmet expectations of people today are driving them into unhealthy attitudes and behaviors. The hope of this book is that by reading and, when appropriate, acting on the information or challenges presented in these chapters some sense of wholeness and balance can come into a stress-filled, overly anxious life.

The key Bible verse driving this project is Luke 2:52; *"Jesus grew in wisdom and in stature and in favor with God and all the people."* (New Living Translation) Jesus had to deal with his own sets of expectations and pressures and this verse shows four distinct growth areas in his life. In this book we want to speak into all parts of a person's life including intellect, physical growth and health, a spiritual dimension of life, and the ever necessary social aspect as well.

I am a pastor and a teacher, not a certified counselor (although some of the contributors to this book are) therefore when words such as stress, anxiety and even depression are used it will generally be more from a nonprofessional's perspective not a clinical description.

THE FORMAT

The writer of each chapter will cover some sort of expertise in their field as it relates to holistic health. Holistic is defined for our purpose as dealing with all aspects of life including the mind, body and spirit. Stories will be told, information will be shared and opportunities for change will be included. Each chapter ends with a practical challenge and some questions for you to consider. You don't need to read this book start to finish. Peruse the contents and choose a chapter that inspires you or reflects a need in your life right now. Then go from there. I hope you will take advantage of these great writers and find your way through this anxious life and into a calmer, more controlled day-to-day existence!

You Got This!

Chapter 1

WHO AM I?

Finding Identity in Christ

By Matthew Godshall

In the world of real estate the mantra, "Location, location, location," reminds potential home buyers that the price of a house is primarily determined by its location. Where a home is located impacts its value more so than its size and condition—a discouraging reality for anyone moving from Louisville, Kentucky to Sacramento, California (which I have personally experienced), but an encouraging reality for anyone moving from New York City to Boise, Idaho.

While the real estate mantra does express a truth regarding the price of a home, it also taps into a deeper, more significant truth regarding the value of location. This truth can be expressed by the mantra, "location shapes our identity." *Who we are* (identity) is inseparably connected to *where we are* (location). In other words, *where* I live (country, state, city, neighborhood), *where* I work, *where* I go to school, and *where* I spend my free time (gym, nature, theater, concerts, etc.) determine who I am. Location and identity are so closely associated that we rarely consciously consider their relationship, even though subconsciously we are constantly integrating them: "I am an American," "I am a Chicago Bears fan," "I am an employee of Starbucks," "I am a member of my local gym." Location has shaped and is shaping my identity, and the same is true for you.

The overarching story of the Bible is about three things. First, it's about finding our identity as human beings. The second focuses on the way our identity has been and continues to be distorted by sin. Third and most important is what the Creator God has done, is doing and will do to restore us to our true identity.

> The Bible is about three things...identity, distortion, and restoration.

As this story unfolds from Genesis through Revelation, the biblical writers often make a close connection between identity and location. For example, the fundamental identity of human beings as *"the image and likeness"* of God (Gen. 1:26) is connected with their location in the Garden of Eden (Gen. 2); and when human beings become broken reflections of the Creator (Gen. 3), their location outside the Garden corresponds to this broken identity. The restoration of human beings begins with the family of Abraham and climaxes in the person of Jesus, Israel's Messiah; and, for both the nation of Israel and Jesus, location in the "Promised Land" is inseparable from their identity-restoring mission. Even when the biblical writers provide us with glimpses of the future resolution to God's identity-restoring work, there is always an emphasis on location: we will receive new bodies (resurrection) so that we can live *in* God's new creation

However, what about *now*? If we are followers of Jesus, we don't currently live *in* the Garden of Eden, most of us don't live *in* Israel/Palestine, and we are definitely not yet living *in* the new creation. Does location play an identity-shaping role for those of us who are currently in process of being restored into the image and likeness of God? Yes, it does.

The apostle Paul strives to shape the imagination of his readers so that they see themselves as having a new location. Repeatedly in his thirteen letters, he refers to the new location believers have as "in Christ." Yes, they were living "in Galatia" or "in Corinth," but they were ultimately living "in Christ" — a location that transcends provinces and cities or zip codes and national borders. If we are followers of Jesus, this is our ultimate location as well, and this location ought to be the one that shapes our identity more so than where our home is located, where we work, where we go to school, and where we spend our free time. Let's explore what Paul teaches about our ultimate location in his letter to the Christians in Ephesus.

RELOCATING THE CHRISTIANS IN EPHESUS
The first occurrence of the phrase "in Christ" (or "in Christ Jesus") is found in the opening greeting to the Ephesian Christians:

> *Paul, an apostle of Christ Jesus by the will of God,*
> *to the saints who are in Ephesus*
> *and are faithful in Christ Jesus.* (Ephesians 1:1, ESV)

This initial use of the phrase *in Christ* helps us to interpret its meaning throughout the letter. By paralleling "in Christ Jesus" with "in Ephesus," it is clear that Paul is thinking in terms of location. Their new, or ultimate, location of being "in Christ" does not remove them from their present, everyday context of being "in Ephesus." Rather, they are "in Christ" while they are "in Ephesus." Paul's vision of our new location is not a mystical union or utopian dream of escaping the world; rather, our new location grounds us as we live *in* our countries, states, neighborhoods, places of work and schools.

RELOCATING THE EPHESIAN CHRISTIANS IN GOD'S STORY

Every location has a story. In Ephesians 1:20-23 Paul briefly tells the story of what God has done to triumph over the forces of evil that plague his good world and to restore all things under his life-giving rule. In these short verses Paul makes some radical claims: God has raised Jesus from death, placed Jesus on the throne of the universe, all powers (especially those unseen forces of evil the New Testament refers to as "demons") are subject to Jesus' authority and Jesus is the "head" over all things.

However, how do we know these things are true? As we look at the world around us, it sure does not look like God has triumphed over the forces of evil and is in the process of restoring all things! I believe Paul anticipated this important question, although we oftentimes miss the answer he provides because of the chapter division in our English Bible. Immediately after making these radical claims, chapter 2 begins with the words "And you...."

How do we know God has triumphed over the forces of evil that plague his good world? Because *you* once were dead in your sins and living according to the destructive practices of this world and under the influence of the evil one himself (2:1-3). However because of God's great love for you, he made you alive with Christ, raised you up with Christ and seated you with Christ in the heavenly places *in Christ Jesus*. In addition, in the future, God will continue to demonstrate his abundant grace toward us *in Christ Jesus* (2:4-7), which means you are God's handiwork created *in Christ Jesus* for good works (2:8-10).

Speaking to the Ephesian Christians, Paul brings them into the evil-triumphing, creation-restoring story of God. Paul's logic implies that the Ephesian Christians are the evidence of God's triumphal and restoring work. As we experience freedom from sin's power, the beauty of new life with God, and the joy of practicing the "good works" He has for us, we actually become the proof of God's triumph over evil and the evidence that his plan to restore all things has begun. Location shapes our identity!

RELOCATING OUR IDENTITY "IN CHRIST"

New Testament scholar Timothy Gombis writes, "We are now 'in Christ,' which becomes our fundamental identity, opening up for us an entirely new range of options for behaviors, relationships, patterns of thought and speech and the future trajectory of our lives."[4] The following list highlights some of the specific ways our new location provides us with a new identity according to Ephesians. In Christ you are:

- chosen by God and adopted as His child (1:4-5)

- redeemed, forgiven and lavished with His grace (1:7-8)
- sealed with the Holy Spirit who is the down payment of your future inheritance — life in God's kingdom (1:13-14; 5:5)
- no longer dead in your sins and enslaved to self-destructive habits and ways of thinking (2:1-3)
- raised from death, made alive and seated with Christ in the heavenly places (2:3-6)
- a forever recipient of God's inexhaustible grace (2:7)
- God's handiwork, beautifully created and designed for "good works" (2:10)
- a member of God's family and a full citizen of his kingdom (2:11-22)
- being restored into the likeness of Christ (4:15)
- a beloved child of God and are being restored to imitate God by reflecting his self-giving, sacrificial love (5:1)

TRUE IDENTITY

No matter where we live, work, go to school, and spend our free time, we are ultimately "in Christ." This is our new location that provides us with our new, in fact, true identity. In Christ, we are being restored to be men and women who accurately and appropriately reflect God in our relationships with each other and in the ways we care for God's world. In Christ we've been brought into God's story and are experiencing his saving grace which frees us *from* sin's power and *for* becoming the people He's made us to be. Location shapes our identity, and this is good news!

THE CHALLENGE

Henri Nouwen once observed three lies of identity: I am what I have, I am what I do, and I am what other people say or think about me.[5] When I pause to reflect on these lies, I find that I am most susceptible to them when I lose sight of my ultimate location as "in Christ". Over the next week, take some time to reflect on some of the obvious or subtle ways that you are embracing these three lies of identity. Then, take some time to rewrite Nouwen's quote into three truths of your identity in Christ using some of the ideas Paul shares in Ephesians: I am _____, I am _____, and I am _____.

TO THINK ABOUT...

1. How has my location shaped my identity (for better or worse)?

2. How does interpreting the phrase "in Christ" as a reference to my new, ultimate location differ from previous ways I've understood this idea?

3. How might reflecting upon my new location better help me to navigate the three lies of identity?

Chapter 2

SPIRITUAL MUSCLES

Developing a Disciplined Rhythm

By Mark Moore

By the time I was a junior in college I was tired of being a Christian. I grew up in a wonderfully loving Christian home. I attended a small private Christian school from preschool through High School. I was then at a Christian Liberal Arts University. I had been in church my whole life. Sunday school, vacation Bible school, youth group, and summer camps. If the church offered it I was there. I was an all-around "good" kid but by the age of 20 my faith had dried up. It was easy for me to affirm the core doctrines of the church: God the Father as maker of heaven and earth, Jesus as his only begotten Son, the empowering Spirit. I knew the right answers but I also knew there was something missing. On a cold Midwest afternoon in February in the solitude of my off-campus apartment, I realized that I was spiritually dry, because I was not doing anything with my faith. My faith had been merely belief without action, or a bare minimum of action. My daily schedule looked no different because of my faith, save for a few short prayers before meals and at bedtime. I wanted more. I wanted more than mere belief. I wanted my life to be oriented toward and around God.

Not only did I want more, I needed more for my own personal well-being. My inaction had caused a severe crisis of faith that was affecting my mental and physical health.[6] I felt inauthentic. I called myself a Christian. I enjoyed a wonderful Christian heritage. I was surrounded by all things God, but I had no consistent connection *with* God. It was in the midst of this crisis that I was introduced to the spiritual disciplines. The spiritual disciplines provided the action I needed. They were changes I could make to my daily life that structured my life around my faith. For too long my faith had been a mere add on to my everyday life.

DISCIPLINE AND MAGICAL THINKING

Dallas Willard states, "There is much magical thinking going on in Evangelicalism: that if we just hear good teaching long enough and believe it, it will transform our life."[7] I was under the impression that because I was raised in a Christian home, attended a Christian primary school and University; by proxy I would have a flourishing spiritual life. I easily fell into the trap that Willard notes here. I also fell into the trap of grace. Now hear me out on this. Growing up in a strong tradition of grace and faith alone, there was an unspoken discouragement of anything that was too structured, too calculated. Not wanting to "earn" salvation many evangelical churches steered away from any spiritual practice that could be viewed as a work. As my faith dried up I knew I needed action. I needed some structure and discipline.

I define spiritual discipline as an action that you do (i.e. fast, pray, meditate, study) which develops a habit of the heart, which in turn provides strength to accomplish something you cannot readily do (i.e. love your enemy, be patient with a messy roommate, find peace in the midst of a stressful time of life). It is through discipline that we grow and change into the type of people God is calling us to be.

In his second letter to Timothy, the apostle Paul uses three metaphors to depict a disciplined spiritual life: the athlete, the soldier, and the farmer (2 Tim 2:3-6). Each of these three lives a life that is decidedly marked by discipline. The agricultural metaphor of a farmer might be the least familiar to many but not to me. I had the privilege of watching my grandfather, a fourth-generation farmer. No employer told him when to be at work. No timecard needed punching. No vacation or sick days were tracked. Morning after morning he rose with sun and worked in the fields or in the barn. He rested in the mid-afternoon and then worked until sunset. He maintained his equipment each winter in order to be prepared to plant at just the right time in the spring. He had a rhythmed and disciplined life that ensured food on the table each harvest. Paul compares this with the spiritual life. Spiritual vitality requires rhythm and discipline.

The athletic imagery is perhaps the most familiar one of Paul's three metaphors. Growing up I had posters on my wall of a few of my favorite professional athletes: Ozzie Smith, hall of fame shortstop for the St. Louis Cardinals, leaping in the air turning a double play, and Michael Jordan soaring from the free throw line in the

1988 dunk contest.[8] It was easy as a child to idolize these athletes and focus on their extreme talent. What did not make the posters, though, were the hours of hard work and dedication it took for them to be able perform at such a high level. The same is true for the spiritual life. It is easy to idolize the spiritual giants in our lives but if we looked closely at their lives we would see the key to their depth in simple and intentional practices.

All three of these metaphors share something in common: intentionality. One is not accidentally a great athlete, soldier, or farmer. Intentionality has been a word

> "Spend one hour a day adoring your Lord and never do anything which you know is wrong."
> Mother Teresa

that I have been drawn to repeatedly in my spiritual life. I was unsatisfied with living an unintentional Christian life. The spiritual disciplines provided time-tested practices that intentionally focused my spiritual life. Henri Nouwen once asked Mother Teresa the key to the spiritual life. She responded, "Spend one hour a day adoring your Lord and never do anything which you know is wrong."[9] The key to her amazing life was simply intentional time in prayer, not requesting anything but rather adoring.

FINDING YOUR RHYTHM

Whether you are spiritually dry or desiring a hunger for more depth, now is the perfect time to begin to develop an intentional rhythm for your spiritual life. Spiritual health is a key dimension of overall health, and the habits you develop now will remain with you for years to come, for better or worse. If you develop the practices of a deep and meaningful spiritual life, you will lay a foundation upon which a life of purpose and peace can be built. To begin finding your own spiritual rhythm here is some advice that I found helpful.

Start Small

A frequent mistake that many people make in the spiritual life is trying to do too much too quickly. We are inspired by Mother Teresa's practice and we attempt to start with one hour of prayer or meditation. When that hour drags and feels like five hours we get discouraged. Our discouragement demotivates us the next day when looking at that hour.

When I began exploring the spiritual disciplines my junior year, particularly the disciplines of prayer and study, I began with fifteen minutes a day. In those fifteen minutes I read one verse or short passage and silently prayed the rest of the time. After a month or so the habit of dedicating time to prayer and study began to form and the timeframe began to grow.

The habit continues to this day and I find I live for the thirty minutes I dedicate to it each morning. I also began to add on the disciplines of fasting, simplicity, and service but those did not happen all at once.

Explore Variety

I encourage you to explore and experiment with the vast variety of disciplines that are available. The spiritual life is not a one size fits all. You may find that one particular discipline does nothing for you while another draws you closer to the heart of God and gives you life. Richard Foster, in *Celebration of Discipline*, offers three categories of disciplines: inward, outward, and corporate.[10] Some inward disciplines are meditation, prayer, fasting, and study. Outward disciplines are solitude, submission, simplicity, and service. The corporate disciplines include confession, worship, guidance, and celebration.[11] I encourage you to choose one from these categories and experiment. If nothing happens simply choose another. There is no right formula.

Be Consistent
The key to the spiritual life is consistency; it is not a sprint but a marathon. Strive to carve out dedicated time for your spiritual life each day. As you do this more consistently, the time you spend practicing the disciplines will become an invaluable part of your day. Days that you miss this time will feel incomplete. The habits of the spiritual life will grow stronger, until a flourishing spiritual life becomes a part of the natural rhythm of your life.

> *You may find that one particular discipline does nothing for you while another draws you closer to the heart of God.*

THE CHALLENGE

Choose one spiritual discipline listed in this chapter and practice it consistently for two weeks. At the end of that time, process your experience with a friend. Either continue doing what you are doing, add another, or explore a new discipline.

TO THINK ABOUT...

1. How would I characterize my current experience of the spiritual life: vibrant, stagnant, or dying?

2. Do I desire a deeper spiritual life but feel a little lost as to how to attain one?

3. What spiritual disciplines have I tried before? How did it go?

4. What changes will need to occur in order to make the spiritual life a more important part of my daily rhythm?

Chapter 3

UPWARDS

Overcoming Through God's Word

By Derek Zahnd

In November of 2016 Alex Honnold attempted something even professional rock climbers thought impossible.[12] He sought to climb Yosemite's El Capitan, one of the world's most iconic walls, rising some 3000 feet from the valley floor, using just his hands and feet. No ropes, no help. In the pre-dawn darkness, some 600 feet up the nearly vertical rock, Alex shined his headlamp on the cold smooth granite looking for a foothold. His toes had gone numb. His right ankle was stiff and swollen from a severe sprain. Two months earlier, practicing the climb attached to ropes, he had fallen at just this part of the route. This day, there would be no room for error. Suddenly the valley quiet was broken as a supporter reported, "Alex is bailing." The climb was over.

Ever want to bail?

School is hard. Work is hard. Relationships are complex and demanding. Sometimes life is *tough.* And yet, like Alex, we all have goals and dreams. You may want to develop your mind and skills through a college education. Or, to find someone to share your life with in marriage. Or, to discern how you can contribute to others through a meaningful career. Or, something else entirely.

None of our goals happen automatically; we all face obstacles. So did Alex. On El Capitan, the sun can heat the rock so it burns to the touch; temperatures can plummet below freezing; weather systems can push thermal updrafts against the wall. Bees, frogs and birds sometimes scatter out of crevices. Rocks can give way and tumble downward. Alex would even encounter a roped climber in a pink unicorn suit. Random. Those are the *external obstacles*. Inwardly, climbers like Alex face fear, doubt and fatigue. How we handle obstacles and what becomes of our goals, has much to do with how we prepare.

Alex thought about climbing El Capitan for years. To free solo this vertical rock formation Alex trained himself by climbing El Capitan with ropes some fifty times. He spent hundreds of hours attached to ropes working on a difficult stretch called Freeblast. Other sections of the wall he practiced dozens

> *"In a real sense, I performed the hard work of that free solo during the days leading up to it."* Alex Honnold

of times. He choreographed the climb, memorizing thousands of challenging hand and foot sequences. While we may aspire to different goals than Alex, we also help ourselves by preparation. As Christ followers, we have a source of balance, stamina and strength: The Word of God.

READING THE WORD OF GOD
One of the most effective things we can do to overcome obstacles and meet goals is to develop the habit of reading

the Word of God each day. However, even in daily Bible reading, there are obstacles. We can think:

- "I come from a Christian family. I'm good."
- "I grew up in church. I've heard it all already."
- "I don't need to read the Bible on my own. I am at a Christian school."
- "I go to chapel. Why spend even *more* time on this?"
- "I study the Bible in class. Why would I read it on my own? Anyway, I don't have time."

Yet we know, what is *outside* us does not influence us nearly as much as what is *inside* us. Each one of us is responsible for the care of our own soul.[13] There is no shortage of helpful spiritual pathways. God can speak to us through worship music, thoughtful Christian books, service, nature, our friends and other means.[14] However, there is no substitute for the Word of God.

According to a Barna study, most Americans believe the Bible is either the actual word of God (24%) or the inspired word of God with no errors (30%).[15] Even though a majority of Americans may hold a 'high' view of Scripture, that doesn't mean a majority reads it -- at least, not very often. Three out of five Americans say they wished they spent more time reading the Bible.

Every morning, you and I have the opportunity to begin the day reading God's Word. There is no better source for inspiration and encouragement, truth and wisdom. You will read many books in college. However, New Testament scholar Mark Strauss reminds us, "The

Bible is the most revered, respected and celebrated book of all time."[16]

My habit is to read the Word of God on The Bible App on my phone during breakfast. I usually read a few chapters, highlighting passages that speak to me. Through The Bible App friends and family can comment back to me on those verses. You will want to pick a solid translation that is easy to understand; many people like the NIV or ESV. In addition, don't be afraid to use the Table of Contents to find a book. When do you read the Word of God?

> "It ain't those parts of the Bible that I can't understand that bothers me, it is the parts I do understand." Mark Twain

MEMORIZING THE WORD OF GOD

Even as Alex memorized complex physical maneuvers for his climb, we can memorize key passages of the Word of God. We live in the Technology/Innovation Age. Accessing information is not our problem, but being shaped by the right information often is. Our minds conform to what they concentrate upon. In choosing to memorize Scripture we shape our minds, and thereby affect our behavior.

Psalm 119:11 says, *"I have hidden your word in my heart that I might not sin against you."* (NIV) Some of my friends memorize a verse a week from the sermon at church. As we gather for meals or meetings, we share the reference, the text word-perfect, the reference again, and then a comment on what it means to us. What a comfort, when facing a challenge, to reflect on memorized Scripture. It's a secure place to hang on to. When do you memorize the Word of God?

Our culture prizes speed. We eat fast food and look for ever-faster replies to our texts and emails. Yet memorizing the Word of God slows us down. It reminds us we are looking at something eternal. The Word of God came before us and will be here long after us. Memorizing a bit of it brings perspective to the concerns of the day.

KNOWING THE WORD OF GOD: JESUS

The greatest benefit of reading and memorizing the written Word of God is knowing Jesus Christ, the Word of God incarnate, in the flesh. John 1:1 says, *"In the beginning was the Word, and the Word was with God, and the Word was God."* (NIV) Speaking about Jesus, Revelation 19:13 says, *"His name is the Word of God."* (NIV) Kevin Vanhoozer a New Testament scholar says, "It is only in Scripture that we come to know, and be known, by Him who is the way, the truth, and the life." [17]

Seven months after quitting, on June 3, 2017, Alex started the climb again. This time he finished, nearly four hours later, standing atop El Capitan. What goals and dreams has God called you to pursue? What obstacles must be overcome?

Whatever your answer, you can be strengthened and encouraged, equipped and supported by the Word of God. Make a habit of reading and memorizing the Word of God. Along the way, you will come to know the Incarnate Word of God, Jesus Christ, better too.

THE CHALLENGE

Consider downloading and use The Bible App on your phone at youversion.com. Check out biblegateway.com for study guides and commentaries. Take some time to reflect on these verses about God's Word: Psalm 19:7-9, Psalm 119:105, John 17:7, Matthew 4:4, Romans 15:4, 2 Timothy 3:16-17. Finally, use the Navigators Topical Memory System to memorize a verse a week with a friend.[18]

TO THINK ABOUT...

1. What do I really want out of life? What are my goals and dreams?

2. How could reading and memorizing the Word of God help me overcome obstacles I face?

3. How could I start to read the Word of God daily?

4. With whom could I begin to memorize a verse a week?

Chapter 4

TURN DOWN THE VOLUME!

Restoring Quiet Times

By Ryan P. Murphy

I want to encourage you to stop right now and just listen for a moment…

What sounds do you hear? Do you hear the subtle hum of an air conditioner, the purr of a computer hard drive, the roar of the cars outside, or the melodies from your wireless earphones? Chances are, you have gotten so used to the noises that you didn't even realize they were there.

Since the Industrial Revolution, our world has gradually turned from the pastoral quietness of nature to honks, hums, and the constant noise of various technologies. I want to suggest in this chapter that the ambient noise of the 21st century has become so ubiquitous or ever-present, that many followers of Jesus have accidentally replaced

> Many followers of Jesus have accidentally replaced the still, small voice of the Spirit for the hustle and bustle of the technological world around them.

the still, small voice of the Spirit for the hustle and bustle of the technological world around them. What would it look like to turn down this ambient noise and spend time to listen to that still, small voice of the Holy Spirit instead? How would that change your life? Your stress levels?

Your emotional state of joy and peace throughout the day?

IS OUR WORLD GETTING LOUDER?

Recently, researchers for the Environmental Health Perspectives journal reported that over 104 million individuals "were at risk of noise-induced hearing loss" and that "tens of millions more" are at risk of "other noise-related health effects" such as heart disease.[19] That's over a third of the population of the United States at a serious noise-related health risk!

By all accounts, with the increase of electronic noises from music to machines, to rapidly expanding cities, to jet-aircraft, our world is getting noisier. In 1970, R. Murray Shafer announced the World Soundscape Project as a response to the post-war increase in noise coupled with the new ability to record sounds at relatively high-fidelity for the purpose of study. In the compilation produced by more recent efforts of this research group, *Sonic Experience*, the editors describe the increasingly ubiquitous noises of the modern world — sounds which are so ever-present that they are "characterized by the fact that we forget them and no longer hear them."[20] Imagine the difference between walking in nature, and hearing every small sound from the leaves crunching to the birds chirping, to walking in a crowded city, where every sound becomes so common we tune it out.

Have you ever walked through a shopping mall or a large department store, and heard the same music, at practically the same volume throughout the store? It becomes the background noise to your shopping experience, and is so omnipresent you usually forget it is there. That is *ubiquitous* noise — "a presence whose center is everywhere and whose circumference is nowhere." This, Shafer notes with shockingly relevant insight, "is how the medieval theologians defined God" — omnipresent. He goes on to say that at one point in Western history, the only pervasive sound was the church bells in the center of a town, ringing every hour, but now this solitary omnipresent sound has been replaced by "traffic noise and amplified pop music." [21]

> *Ubiquitous noise — a presence whose center is everywhere and whose circumference is nowhere.*

Is it possible that the regular noise of church bells of Western society has been replaced by the noise of machines? That the type of sound that once called us to worship God has now been replaced by background music at a shopping mall, driving us to another kind of worship entirely?

HOW DID JESUS RESPOND TO THE NOISE?

The Gospel of Mark records a story where Jesus encouraged his disciples to rest for a while because so many people were coming and going to them for ministry. He writes; *"The apostles gathered around Jesus, and told him all that they had done and taught. He said to them, 'Come away to a deserted place all by yourselves and rest a while.' For many were coming and going, and they had no leisure even to eat. And they went away in the boat to a deserted place by themselves."* (Mark 6:30-32 NRSV)

In fact, this is one consistent similarity between all the Gospel authors — they all record Jesus withdrawing from the noise of life to pray in silence and solitude! *"Now when Jesus heard this he withdrew from there in a boat to a deserted place by himself."* (Matthew 14:13a NRSV) *"But now more than ever the word about Jesus spread abroad; many crowds would gather to hear him and to be cured of their diseases. But he would withdraw to deserted places to pray."* (Luke 5:15-16 NRSV) *"But after his brothers had gone to the festival, then he also went, not publicly but as it were in secret."* (John 7:10 NRSV)

Later, in John 15, Jesus leaves some "last instructions" before his crucifixion, resurrection, and ascension. Some of his most important last words to his disciples are these: *"Abide in me as I abide in you. Just as the branch cannot bear fruit by itself unless it abides in the vine, neither can you unless you abide in me."* (John 15:4 NRSV)

Dallas Willard, a famous Christian philosopher, once described his life as a disciple of Jesus by saying; "I am learning from Him how to lead my life in the Kingdom of the Heavens as He would lead my life if he were I." [22] He describes a process of discipleship as a process of apprenticeship to Jesus — learning how Jesus would live if He were us.

My question is this — how would Jesus live if He were surrounded by the ubiquitous technological noise of the 21st century? If the crowds and noise of ministry in Jesus's own time caused Him to withdraw to "desolate places," how much more should we as disciples of Jesus withdraw from our noisy world?

HOW HAS THE CHURCH RESPONDED TO THE NOISE?

Throughout church history, various followers of Jesus have proposed different ways to retreat from the noise. The church fathers practiced silence & solitude, *lectio divina*, the contemplative reading of Scripture, fasting, and other spiritual disciplines that have continued through the centuries.

In the nineteenth century, followers of Jesus in the Keswick movement developed a new sort of spiritual discipline which they described as the "Morning Watch," a personal prayer time based on a belief in the need to fight demonic powers for a successful ministry. In 1880, pastor A.B. Simpson discovered the Quaker practice of "Listening Prayer" and developed a new spiritual discipline loosely based on these Morning Watches — Quiet Times. Increasingly, the Morning Watch fell out of practice and was replaced by Quiet Times, these personal times of reflection and prayer, as a response to the busyness of the modern world. These quiet times are now described by one researcher as "the dominant form of evangelical piety today."[23]

Perhaps now, more than ever, there is a need for modern-day followers of Jesus to withdraw from the hustle and bustle, the ubiquitous technological noise, to pray. What we need is a return to Quiet Times.

WHAT IS OUR RESPONSE TO THE NOISE?

So how can we practically do this? Just as the Church responded to the increasing modernization with the development of a "Quiet Time," we all the more have an opportunity to respond to a new development — technology. What are ways that we as 21st century disciples of Jesus can respond to the increase of noise that comes specifically from technology?

> "The secret to praying is praying in secret."
> Leonard Ravenhill

I want to suggest that just as Jesus withdrew from the crowds to find a space where He was by himself, there is an opportunity for us as well to withdraw from the technology that has filled our lives. Here are four possible ways to withdraw from the noise of technology to engage with God in a fresh way:

1. Put your phone on "Do Not Disturb" and close your laptop for 15 minutes and use that time to read the Bible or reflect in silence.

2. Leave all technology at home and go on a walk outside (yes, even leaving your wireless earphones behind!) and listen to the sounds of nature.

3. Set a timer on your phone for 15 minutes and don't check your phone that entire time.

4. Pull out a real piece of paper and some pens and write down your prayers or reflectively journal what you feel God is speaking to you.

THE CHALLENGE

Do one of these four 21st century spiritual disciplines as soon as possible. Which one sticks out to you the most? Which one challenges you the most? Do that one!

TO THINK ABOUT...

1. What noises in my life have become "ubiquitous" — so present that I don't even notice them?

2. How often is there *no* background noise in my life?

3. What is my biggest obstacle to sitting in silence with the Lord?

4. How can I remove that obstacle this week to spend real quiet time with the Lord?

Chapter 5

I CAN RELATE

Discovering Sacred Pathways

By Kay Llovio

Have you ever played the "Trust Fall" game? It's pretty simple. One person has to fall backwards on purpose while another person catches you. You stand facing away from your partner, make your body go stiff, and give a signal when you are ready to fall. Your partner has to catch you gently and prevent you from hitting the ground. As your confidence grows, the distance between you increases.

Before we do this exercise in my college freshman class, approximately two-thirds of the students believe "Falling would be no problem!" Another three in ten confess they're not sure their partner would catch them. Occasionally, one will admit, "No way!"

Afterwards, we discuss their experiences of security and risk in the exercise:

- Did you have any hesitation before falling?
- How did you feel having to rely on others to support you?
- Can you relate this challenge to a time when you have had to rely on others?

TRUSTING GOD

Trusting God is a lot like trusting another human being. In our Trust Fall analogy, trust is a factor of our knowledge of both ourselves and the other person. It is usually easier for students to trust someone they know, less so someone they just met a week earlier at a college orientation. That makes sense. It is the same with God. You cannot "fall into His arms" if you are not confident in His ability and willingness to catch you, or if you want or need to retain control.

> "Never be afraid to trust an unknown future to a known God."
> Corrie Ten Boom

How can we move our relationship with God beyond a superficial level? How can we develop intimacy with God? The main factor that acts as a catalyst in any relationship development is proper self-disclosure, or knowing and revealing one's personality and character, as Altman and Taylor propose in Social Penetration Theory.[24]

In *Faith: Security and Risk*, Richard W. Kropf diagrams faith as the growing confidence that emerges from a person's search for ultimate meaning in life.[25] Trusting God begins with sharing oneself with who you think God is and waiting in expectation before sharing more. At the same time, we need to be open to increasing our understanding of God as He reveals himself. Some people call this "letting God out of the box" of our limited understanding (Isaiah 55:8-9).

Unsure of how you currently view God? Try drawing a picture of Him, of what comes to your mind when you hear the word "God." Some of us may find we have a negative view of God, perhaps growing up with God and Christ as curse words. Don't censor your artistic expression from the subconscious - it may reveal more than you expect.

What's your view of yourself? Positive or negative? Strengths and weaknesses? Talents? Are you confident that God designed each of us as a unique individual and never intended a one-size-fits-all notion of spirituality? Perhaps you have been trying to walk in someone else's shoes as you approach God.

SACRED PATHWAYS

"I get so bored when I have to sit at a desk and do my Bible devotional," Jeff expressed. "But, I love taking long walks and just talking to God, like a good friend."

When missionary Eric Liddell accidentally missed a church prayer meeting because of his running, his sister accused him of no longer caring about God. Eric tells her, "I believe that God made me for a purpose. But He also made me fast, and when I run, I feel His pleasure."[26]

Writer Victor Hugo shares, "Music expresses that which cannot be said and on which it is impossible to be silent."

Other chapters in this book will offer insights and advice to deepen your spiritual life. Take note which ones resonate with you and which do not. Author Gary Thomas writes about nine *Sacred Pathways*, which he says describe "the way we relate to God and how we draw near to Him."[27] Thomas offers examples from the life of

Jesus and other Bible characters who approach God in a variety of ways. Viewing God through the experiences of others helps you see Him outside of your 'box.'

Which of the pathways below appeal to you? Like Eric Liddell, you will feel His pleasure most when you run the pathway He designed for *you*.

Intellectuals enjoy the discipline of study, whether a set routine of Bible study or the deeper exploration of theology or church history. The sermon is often the most appealing part of a church service for them. Intellectuals find the deep thoughts of God intriguing and enjoy their Bible classes, as they accept the challenge given by the Apostle Paul to "be transformed by the renewing of your mind" (Romans 12:2).

Naturalists like Jeff love the outdoors, agreeing with the psalmist that *"The heavens declare the glory of God; the skies proclaim the works of his hands"*. (Psalm 19:1 NIV) Whether in the mountains, at the ocean, tending a garden, or walking the backroads of town or city, Naturalists find in creation more than an escape from the indoors. Nature provides a testament to the variety, creativity, and abundance of God.

Sensates engage the five senses of sight, smell, touch, taste, and sound in their worshipful experiences. Perhaps it is in playing music or singing, contemplating art or drawing, lighting candles or waving palm branches, eating matzah or bitter herbs. Sensates experience God more when their senses come alive (Revelation 1). How often do the church services you attend incorporate all five senses?

Ascetics, on the other hand, often deny the distractions of the senses by loving God in solitude and simplicity. A modern John the Baptist might enjoy a personal retreat or period of fasting from food, speaking, social media, or digital entertainment. Ascetics make time to *"Be still, and know that I am God"*. (Psalm 46:10 NIV)

Traditionalists appreciate the stability of routine and ritual, finding a connection to centuries of Christian practice though scheduled prayer and scripture memorization, regular celebrations and observances like communion (Luke 4:16). Or, you might go to a church that follows the liturgical calendar and its seasons – from the Advent of Christ to Pentecost and beyond – to instruct believers in the life of Christ and the Church.

Enthusiasts prefer "to let go and experience God on the precipice of excitement and awe"[28] through supernatural expectancy in dreams,

> *"This is the day the Lord hath made; let us rejoice and be glad in it." Psalm 118:24*

prayer, and worship. They expect God to break into our world today and make known His presence and will. In turn, they respond like King David, with outbursts of joy and celebration (1 Chronicles 13:8).

Contemplatives express their passionate love for God differently, by gazing in the face of their lover, Christ (Deuteronomy 33:12; Luke 10:42). An intense awareness of the presence of Christ is fostered through focused quiet prayer that allows for prayerful reflection and submission. While contemplatives seem to bathe in

God's love, they can be misunderstood by those who experience God with a different focus.

Caregivers walk in the footsteps of Jesus by caring for the poor, the sick, the needy, the imprisoned. If you find yourself helping a friend through a personal crisis, volunteering in your community, watching children for tired parents, or feeding the homeless, your compassion is speaking God's love to the world (Matthew 14:14).

Activists confront injustice through prayer, intercession, and social reform. As Jesus cleansed the temple of the moneychangers (Mark 11:15-19), activists speak up on behalf of those less fortunate and often fight their battles in two realms to restore both social and spiritual order. A quiet form of activism is prayer-walking, where believers "pray on site with insight" that God's will be done on earth as it is in heaven.

THE CHALLENGE

As you read these brief descriptions, more than one pathway may have sounded like a fit with your personality, your spiritual gifts, and your strengths. In fact, you might feel a bit like *all* of them describe you! So that you can strip aside the one-size-fits-all notion of spirituality and find your pathways, Thomas' book, *Sacred Pathways*, includes questions like the ones below to help you know and reveal your spiritual wiring.[29] Or, you could simply rest in the knowledge that God has uniquely created you to be in relationship with Him and enjoy the journey!

TO THINK ABOUT...

1. Where and when do you I closest to God? When do I feel His pleasure?

2. What is my favorite way to picture God? Are there any images of God that I find difficult to contemplate? Why do I think that is?

3. What would I guess are my primary pathways? Have I ever thought of them in this light before?

4. Do any of the other pathways intrigue me enough to want to explore and develop them?

Chapter 6

DON'T WORRY - BE HAPPY!

Learning to Seek First the Kingdom

By Fritz Moga

Mad Magazine is an American humor magazine founded in 1952. The magazine offers satire on all aspects of American life and pop culture, politics, entertainment, and public figures. Alfred E. Neuman is the fictional mascot of *Mad* magazine. Since his debut in *Mad*, Neuman's likeness, distinguished by jug ears, a missing front tooth, and one eye slightly lower than the other, has graced the cover of all but a handful of the magazine's 500 issues. Editor Harvey Kurtzman first spotted the image on a postcard pinned to the office bulletin board of another magazine. "It was a face that didn't have a care in the world, except mischief".[30]

He is typically the focal point of the magazine's cover, with his face often replacing a celebrity or character that is being teased in the issue. Alfred E. Neuman quotes:

- *"A plastic surgeon's office is the only place where no one gets offended when you pick your nose!"*
- *"How come we choose from just two people for President, and fifty for Miss America?"*
- *"Most people are so lazy, they don't even exercise good judgment!"*
- *"If opera is entertainment, then falling off a roof is transportation!"*[31]

Alfred E. Neuman's signature phrase is "What, me worry?" I don't know if Neuman's lack of concern is ignorance of the world around him or a Christian perspective but he is our "poster boy" for today's chapter! If you could pull up or out a Bible and read Matthew chapter 6, verses 25-34 (NIV) it will greatly assist your understanding of the rest of this chapter.

Three times in the Matthew passage, Jesus tells us not to worry (v. 25, 31, 34). Jesus just finished speaking about materialism so assuredly He is still responding to this issue in life. Jesus realized that when we focus on how much "stuff" we should have it leads to anxiety. If this was a message that was needed then it is certainly a message needed even more now.

STATISTICS ON WORRYING

According to the Anxiety Disorders Association of America: Anxiety disorders are the most common mental illness in the U.S., affecting 40 million adults in the United States age 18 and older. Anxiety disorders cost the U.S. more than $42 billion a year, almost one-third of the country's $148 billion total mental health bill.[32]

> We take sleeping pills to go to sleep and gulp down caffeine in the morning to wake us up.

People with an anxiety disorder are three to five times more likely to go to the doctor and six times more likely to be hospitalized for psychiatric disorders than those who do not suffer from anxiety disorders.[33] *(See the chapter on the Giants of Anxiety and Depression for more information on this subject).* Although medications won't cure anxiety they can keep the symptoms under control and enable someone to lead a normal, fulfilling life. Even so we take sleeping pills to go to sleep and gulp down caffeine in the morning to wake us up. People are running to counselors by the millions hoping they can help take away some of the stress and worry from their lives.

We worry a lot! *Before you read on...take a minute and write down the things that cause you to worry.* Start with the big stuff (i.e., your future!) and work your way down to the everyday little things that bother you and you find yourself concerned or fretting about.

There is a difference between worry and concern. We are to be concerned about our spiritual walk, we are to care for others and be disturbed about injustice and poverty in the world. However, more often than not our worry is self-centered and has at its root a lack of trust in God. Here are a couple questions to help process your thoughts and the Matthew Bible verse.

What do you do when you find yourself worrying?

According to Matthew 6:25-34 what kinds of things are we NOT to worry about?

In Matthew 6:25-34 why are we not to worry about these things?

"Look at the birds" (v. 26)

If you were to really take a good look at birds what would you notice? It's a pretty simple life. They fly around, eat when they are hungry, chase one another and none of them seem to be worrying.

"And why do you worry about clothes? See how the lilies of the field grow. They do not labor or spin." (v. 28)

Since God takes care of the inanimate flowers, which are beautiful for a short time and then gone, how much more will he take care of us.

"Is not life more important than food, and the body more important than clothes?" (v. 25b)

If we cannot get over our selfish and materialistic attitudes and rely on God then Jesus is speaking to us when He says; *"O you of little faith"* (v. 31b).

Again, it doesn't mean we aren't concerned when we lose a job or our car breaks down. It does mean that we take a different outlook on the situation. God is not calling us to laziness but to trust.

WHAT ARE WE TO DO INSTEAD?

The world offers all kinds of ideas on how to get over worrying so much. It includes serving others, not sweating decisions, spending well, joining a group, and the encouragement to stop dwelling on the things you can't change and being grateful for what you do have! Certainly all of these things will help us not to worry so much and enjoy life more.

However, for believers we need to look to Scripture for answers and Matthew 6:33 gives us help in learning how to calm down and not worry so much, *"But seek first his kingdom and his righteousness, and all these things will be given to you as well."*

Seek FIRST.

Our first thoughts and actions should be directed toward God. Not humans. Not in response to the media. Not out of our own greed or selfishness...but toward God. The way to do this is wake up every day trusting God in every situation:

When you are trying to make a difficult decision..."Seek First." When you are headed toward a temptation..."Seek First." When you are having a "pity party" about life..."Seek First." When you are anxious and worried about anything..."Seek First."

Make the commitment now to reduce your anxiety by making sure you "SEEK HIM FIRST."

HIS Kingdom.

In the Sermon on the Mount (Matthew Chapters 5-7) we are introduced to how to live as people who believe in God. It includes spreading the good news of Jesus' love, having an understanding that without God we are nothing, living so God would approve of our lifestyle, an effort to focus on others, being a person of prayer, living righteously and showing generosity. Love, generosity and prayer, NOT worry and anxiety should characterize our lives as Kingdom people. How would you characterize your life?

His RIGHTEOUSNESS.

Righteous is defined as *acting in accord with divine or moral law; free from guilt or sin.* We are to seek a life that glorifies God in all we think, say and do.

Don't forget…all this is tied into ANXIETY & WORRY. Worry is caused in great part by not trusting Jesus daily. When we live for Jesus those things we worry about will be taken care of far better than we ever can by using our earthly means!

Look at the last verse, *"Therefore do not worry about tomorrow, for tomorrow will worry about itself. Each day has enough troubles of its own" (v. 34).* Tomorrow or the future will have its troubles. It is unavoidable! By worrying we do nothing but use up our strength and tear down our trust in God. *"Seek first"* is in the present imperative which means we are to be in a continual quest for God's kingdom and godly living. By doing this our focus will be taken off ourselves; what we eat, what we wear, and we will be free from anxiety and worry.

> *"Worry is like a rocking chair: it gives you something to do but doesn't get you anywhere."*
> Erma Bombeck

THE CHALLENGE:
Don't Worry – Be Happy Day. Pick a day and dedicate it to not worrying! Look back on those things you wrote down that cause you to worry. Spend some time in PRAYER. Jot down some ways to not worry about these things for the day. Throughout the day when you begin to worry about anything remind yourself of Matthew 6:33 *"Seek first the Kingdom…"* Spend some time thinking or journaling at the end of the day, how did it go?

TO THINK ABOUT...

1. What from this chapter do I need to remember?

2. When exactly can I plan a "Don't Worry, Be Happy" day?

3. How could I make not worrying a normal part of my life?

Chapter 7

DOWNTIME IS NOT WASTED TIME

Taking Time to Rest

By Libby Backfish

When I ask my college students about the concept of rest, they often laugh and say, "Rest? What's *that*?!" Our lives, from college to retirement, can seem like a succession of one busy and chaotic season in life after another. So what does "rest" look like in such environments, why should we rest, and are some kinds of rest better than others?

WHAT IS REST?

The idea of "rest" in the Bible is broad and deep, and it is fundamentally theological, which is to say that it primarily has to do with God and our relationship to Him. In the deepest sense, the concept of rest is a way of talking about the salvation, security, freedom, and peace that we have in Christ. (Hebrews 4:1-9) When we are in right relationship with God, we can "rest" in the gracious gifts of His salvation. In his *Confessions*, Saint Augustine wrote, "You have made us for yourself, and our hearts are restless until they find rest in you."[34] Psalm 62:1 reflects the same thoughts: *"Truly my soul finds rest in God."* We were made by God, redeemed by God, and so we will

> *Rest?*
> *What's that?*

only truly feel at rest, truly feel "at home," when we live our lives in a trusting relationship with God.

However, rest is not just something that we experience as passive recipients. It is also something that we actively *do* when we make space to step away from our regular activities. In the Old Testament, Israel set apart one day per week, the Sabbath, to rest from their ordinary work so that they could rest in God. Their Sabbaths were times of worship and reflection and fellowship, much like how Christians now set apart the Lord's Day (Sunday) as a special day of rest.

We also set aside certain times and even seasons for rest. Most of us try to incorporate periods of rest in our daily routines, times to recharge our batteries by hanging out with friends, playing a game of basketball, going on a hike, spending devotional time with God and His Word, or taking a quick afternoon nap. Many occupations, such as education, agriculture, and retail, have busy seasons and slower seasons, offering a rhythm of rest and reprieve.

WHY REST?

Why do we need to make space for rest, especially when we have so many other things that we need to do? Aren't the most successful people the ones who *don't* take the time to rest? There are two primary reasons why rest is so important. First, God commands his people to rest. Second, good rest can actually help us to be more productive, more creative, and happier.

God commanded his people Israel to rest on the Sabbath. Christians disagree whether or not this commandment is still applicable, but at the very least, the Sabbath is a symbol of rest and can provide us with some clues as to *why* rest is significant for God's people. There are two different places in the Old Testament where the Ten Commandments are recounted, and each one provides a different reason for the command.

In the first case, Exodus 20:8-11, God explains that Israel must honor the Sabbath day because it is a reflection of God's rest on the seventh day of creation. By remembering the Sabbath, Israel would be remembering and honoring God, which according to Jesus is the greatest commandment (Matthew 22:37-38). In the second case, Deuteronomy 5: 12-15, God explains that the Sabbath rest is for everyone in Israel, including the immigrants and sojourners and servants,

> Not only is rest something Scripture commands us to do, but it is also a gift.

because the Israelites too were once enslaved and immigrants. Remembering the Sabbath was thus a means of maintaining justice, and a way of loving their neighbor, which according to Jesus is the second greatest commandment (Matthew 22:39). Looking at both Sabbath commands together, we can see how Israel's command to rest on the Sabbath also undergirded the two greatest commandments, to love God and to love others.

Not only is rest something that Scripture commands us to do, but it is also a gift and something that enables us to flourish and to do even *better* work. In her book *An*

Oasis in Time: How a Day of Rest Can Save Your Life,
Marilyn Paul discusses how the benefits of rest have been
scientifically proven.[35] Incorporating the right kind of rest
into our patterns of life enables us to recharge and reflect
so that we can resume work with greater creativity,
passion, and efficiency. Rest is also important for
rejuvenating our minds. Poet Wendell Berry describes
this aspect of rest in one of his collected Sabbath poems:

> The mind that comes to rest is tended
> In ways that it cannot intend:
> Is borne, preserved, and comprehended
> By what it cannot comprehend.[36]

What Berry is tapping into here is that our very
bodies were made for rest: we think, work, and grow
when we give our bodies, minds, and souls the rest they
need to thrive.

WHAT KIND OF REST?
However, before you begin to think that the biblical idea
of rest justifies an unlimited amount of Netflix binging or
daily four-hour siestas, we need to understand that there
is a right kind of rest and a wrong kind of rest. "Rest" that
ends up exhausting us more than energizing us is no rest
at all. For example, it might be a lot of fun to play video
games until 3:00 AM, but if it leaves us feeling totally
depleted the next day, is it really rest? Or consider "rest"
that is more about escaping our responsibilities or fears
or anxieties. Does that "rest" leave us feeling any more
secure in our salvation or any more refreshed to face the

work God has given us? Rest does not always need to involve explicitly "Christian" acts of devotion (we are not living in a monastery!) but if our "rest" leaves us feeling more drained or more anxious, then perhaps it's not really the rest we need.

So what is the *right* kind of rest? I suggest that we can judge the quality of our rest by whether or not we feel in some way *better* on the other end of it. Does it recharge our souls to help us feel closer to God so that we can better love him? Does it recharge our compassion and patience with other people so that we can better love our neighbor? Does it recharge our bodies to feel more energized and passionate about resuming our ordinary work and responsibilities? Does it recharge our minds to think more clearly and more biblically about our lives and relationships?

The right rest might also involve knowing when to rest from things that we do not need to do. We often feel pressured to fix broken things, even when those things are outside of our responsibility or control. There is a lot of brokenness in this world that God has called us to fix, but our energies need to be directed to what we *should* and *can* do. We need wisdom to discern what those things are, and we need rest for the energy to do it.

Sometimes, the right kind of rest will even include work, which might sound paradoxical. Jesus told his followers, *"Come to me, all you who are weary and burdened, and I will give you rest"* (Matthew 11:28, NIV). We've already seen how "rest" first and foremost has to do with resting in the salvation that Christ gives us, so Jesus' words make sense. However, in his very next breath, Jesus says, *"Take my yoke upon you and learn from me…my yoke is easy and my burden is light"* (Matthew 11:29-30, NIV). Resting in Jesus meaning taking on His yoke, and taking on His yoke means taking on His work. Does this mean that sometimes rest involves work? I think that it does, but the work described here is not our daily responsibility (the daily "grind" as it were) but rather the work of God. And Jesus tells us that it will be *easy* and *light*, probably because He has made it so and because He has given us the gift of his Holy Spirit, who empowers us to do His work.

THE CHALLENGE
What healthy habits of rest can you start this week? Perhaps just focus on one specific way that you can rest in God, rest from your typical responsibilities, and rest in a way that recharges your energy and love.

TO THINK ABOUT…
1. What do my current habits of rest look like?

2. How could I be more intentional about making space for daily and weekly rest?

3. Do I struggle more to make space for rest, or to practice the right kind of rest?

Chapter 8

WALK, HIKE, BIKE, BREATHE

The Importance of Movement

By Parker Daniells

"A healthy, fit body is the most appropriate home for a vibrant spirit" - Dr. Kenneth Cooper

At a young age, I was introduced to exercise and team sports. Coming from a family that competed in endurance sports produced a culture of waking up at 5am to workout. As I matured, I found that was not a norm for families to do. I can still recall my first duathlon at the age of five. Riding my small Ninja Turtle bike in Laker's warmup pants and Converse shoes. That began my athletic career into swimming, distance running, triathlons, soccer, basketball, volleyball, track & field, surfing and extra-curricular activities like backpacking, fishing, and kayaking.

Of all the years I trained and competed, I was never injured. When I started competing in college, I got my first injury. Up until that point in my life, I had never dealt with any sort of anxiety. I recall talking with the team doctor and athletic trainer about the injury and all of a sudden, I felt this strange pressure in my chest that I could not control. I was having a panic attack. Never to that point in my life had I experienced anything this scary.

Although I've been through other difficult situations, this was the first where control was out of my hands. Even though my injury was small, easily treatable and I would quickly return to workouts within a few weeks, I felt threatened. As if I was losing a part of myself. I did not know how to cope with what I was hearing. I felt helpless.

As I reflect on that experience, I recognize that I never knew what anxiety or stress was because I was physically active every day up to that point. Yes, I lost running for a while but what I really lost was the activity that helped me process my life and stay positive. My emotions and feelings were consistent throughout my life because exercise was consistent in my life.

Most health scientists agree that exercise has a positive effect upon one's physical well-being like heart rate and blood pressure. Evidence shows there are also psychological benefits for individuals that engage in some form of movement. Byrne & Byrne found that exercise could induce anti-depressive properties, combat anxiety, and enhance one's mood.[37]

What type of exercise should one engage in to attain these benefits you may ask? Any! Data has shown that aerobic and non-aerobic activities produce positive effects on the alleviation of depression and improving mood. Movement can also help control weight, provide energy, increase memory, and improve sleep. To achieve these psychological and physiological benefits, we need to go into training.

TRAINING

For as long as I can remember my father, Rick, has shared "Rickisms" with my family. One motto he shouts to my siblings and myself is, "you'll never be smarter, stronger or faster than me." Such a statement can be demoralizing to some, but it inspired me to strive for more. My father would elaborate on what it would take to beat him with specific markers. For example, smarter was to go beyond a Master's degree. Being stronger not only signified lifting more weights but also being stronger mentally. Faster was beating his Ironman personal records.

Being a physically fit person as well as a vice president of sales for a major company, Rick knew that all exercise and no intelligence would produce an individual that could not *finish* the race. Equally, one using all brain and no fitness would probably not even start the race. When deconstructing Rick's motto, it is easy to see a holistic approach in life is necessary for one to complete the race set before us.

As Christians, we often focus more on spiritual training above physical training; the Bible even encourages it, *"For physical training is of some value, but godliness has value for all things, holding promise for both the present life and the life to come."* (1 Timothy 4:8 NIV)

However, to say that spiritual training is more important is not to say that physical fitness does not matter, or that it does not play a role in one's godliness or faith. Dr. Kenneth Cooper's quote at the beginning of this chapter paints a beautiful picture of what God desires our bodies to achieve for a thriving spirit.

Rick's motto goes beyond physical training; it shows a connection between body and soul. To become smarter, faster, and stronger, our physical bodies and spiritual souls must go into strict training (1 Corinthians 9:24-27) and remove anything that contaminates our bodies and spirit. As Paul reminds us in 2 Corinthians 7:1, *"Therefore, since we have these promises, dear friends, let us purify ourselves from everything that contaminates body and spirit, perfecting holiness out of reverence for God."* As Dr. Cooper describes a vibrant spirit, we must engage in movement to feel the intimate relationship between our bodies and soul. To accomplish this, we need to train. We need to stress the body.

DESIRABLE STRESS?

Stress is usually portrayed as undesirable. It is natural to question why exercise is often prescribed as beneficial for health and mood enhancement; especially when exercise is a great deal of work and can be very painful. My definition of exercise here is a physical challenge that is undertaken in graded amounts. What I appreciate about this definition of exercise is its freedom of choice: where (beach, lake, gym, bike path, etc.), when (morning, afternoon, night), how (bike, walk, run, swim, lift, kayak, etc.), how much (weight, time, distance, etc.). With all the options, it provides the exerciser (you) complete control over the outcome. For example, if you want to wake up early for a

> *"We do not stop exercising because we grow old – we grow old because we stop exercising."*
> Kenneth Cooper

30-minute bike ride at a local lake of your choice to watch the sunrise, you have that freedom in exercise to do that. Choosing how you want to exercise helps illicit a positive experience which, in turn, produces a positive mood. Implementing exercise in graded doses allows the body to adapt easier to the physical loads it is taking on. The adaptation process, when done correctly, escapes overtraining and burnout, and has the potential to increase physical fitness and improve one's mood. This level of control and differences in the associated emotions makes *exercise stress* desirable compared to work pressures or an emotionally stressful situation.

There is a clear relationship between exercise and choice. How we interpret a situation as a stressful experience depends on our choice to engage, our motivation, and general feelings about working out. As a coach, I see the importance of choice on a daily basis when planning athlete's workouts. Every single aspect of training required of my athletes has a distinct purpose for their overall goal to improve. Nevertheless, because one athlete does not like weight lifting and believes it is not as important as running sprints, it is viewed as a negative experience. In all reality, the individual does not like weight training because they are not good at it. However, over time, through training, they can improve in their lifting as well as their emotions and mood that surround weights.

So what changed for the athlete over that period of time? In all reality, their perspective. The individual viewed weightlifting as stressful until they began to see its importance in their overall physical development. What I have seen in my years of coaching is that our reactions *to* exercise are often more, important than the exercise itself.

Exercise and building up our fitness level not only requires a lot of work but also some amount of pain. On the other hand, not exercising causes its own pains and physical issues for the future. Physical issues in the future are decided upon by ignoring the challenges or physical problems of the present. Where we once had *choice* to exercise now becomes a *requirement* to improve or sustain our own health issues (diabetes, obesity, strokes, high blood pressure, breathlessness, low energy, stiff joints, and osteoporosis, etc.). Since I know I am going to hurt one way or another, I would much rather be in pain in the present by getting in shape than be suffering in the future because my "home" isn't fit for a thriving spirit.

It makes sense to focus more on spiritual training than physical training but we will not be faithful believers if we ignore our bodies. We should be exalting Christ with our bodies (Philippians 1:20). Scripture encourages us to have a body that will help produce a vibrant spirit that honors God. As Paul wrote to the Thessalonians, our *"whole spirit, soul and body be kept blameless at the coming of our Lord Jesus Christ."* (1 Thessalonians 5:23) Is your soul in a compromised body or in a body that can support your thriving spirit?

THE CHALLENGE

Start somewhere. Start with something. Start now! Choose a simple activity to get your joints moving and your muscles working. Don't take on too much too soon. Maybe just a walk in a park or a simple bike ride on a *flat* path. Then you can add the time, energy and stress to the exercise as you grow into your new practice! Do not wait until your body (and doctors) require you to do something. *Choose* to do it now!

TO THINK ABOUT...

1. How would I characterize my physical heath right now?

2. Where would I like it to be?

3. What stands in the way of beginning to do something (anything) to improve my fitness?

4. What will I do first? When exactly?

Chapter 9

TREE FORTS & PILES OF SNOW

How Being in Nature is a Game Changer

By Fritz Moga

Stop and reflect for a few minutes on the following questions to wrap your head around the topic about to be discussed: How much did you play outside as a kid? Where did you live? What did you do? Did you scamper up the branches of a tree, splash in rivers and lakes, or get the neighborhood together to play hide and seek? Was there any hiking, biking or camping in your childhood?

Here's a follow up question…How much do you play outside now? Do you think things have changed for kids these days? Why? What has changed? What has changed for you?

NATURE DEFICIT DISORDER

In *Last Child in the Woods* author Richard Louv presents us with the concept of Nature Deficit Disorder or NDD. It is defined as the disconnect we have from the natural world around us and the problems that arise from this condition. Such as diminished use of the senses, attention difficulties, and higher rates of physical and emotional illnesses. [38]

We have gone from the utilitarian days of explorers and homesteaders (Lewis & Clark, Davey Crocket and Little House on the Prairie) through the romantic attachment to nature (writers and painters like John Muir and Ansel Adams). We now are in the electronic detachment stage; an increasingly intellectual period with nature, where we want to "save the whales" but don't realize that "boneless" chickens aren't actually chickens without bones!

When I was a young boy, forts and treehouses were the norm for afterschool play. A rugged game of army (often with actual bb guns) was the way to spend an entire Saturday from morning until dark. Now trees are often "off limits" in some parks because of the damage to the bark as kids climb them. I would have to agree with the bumper stickers that say, "Skateboarding is not a crime" although in many parks and communities it actually is!

> "I like to play indoors better 'cause that's where all the electrical outlets are." Paul – a fourth grader from San Diego

Why might this be important and especially as it has to do with our health? We already know through numerous studies that when leisure time is reduced (because of our hectic, busy lifestyle) and we spend more time in front of a screen, television, or computer, obesity is a probable outcome.

WHAT DO THE EXPERTS SAY?

According to recent data just over half of adults nationally, 51.7%, meet the National Physical Activity Guidelines for aerobic activity. In this survey, adults who are physically inactive are those who did not engage in physical activity or exercise during the previous 30 days other than for their regular job.[39]

In one study, parents of children 8 to 12 years old said their children spend three times as many hours with computers and televisions each week as they do playing outside. That same study found that more than half of adults reported spending five hours or less in nature each week, and worse yet they felt satisfied with their meager time spent outside.[40]

Studies suggest that exposure to nature may reduce the symptoms of ADHD and can improve children's cognitive abilities and resistance to negative stress and depression.[41] In addition, those results may be the same for adults.

Mardie Townsend, PhD, associate professor at the School of Health and Social Development at Deakin University in Australia says, "There is mounting evidence that contact with nature has significant positive impacts on mental health. It is associated with reduced levels of stress — which also has huge ramifications for physical health, reduced levels of depression and anxiety, increased resilience, improved self-esteem and increased capacity to engage socially."[42]

Pediatricians now warn that today's children "may be the first generation of Americans since World War II to die at an earlier age than their parents."[43]

WHAT DOES THE BIBLE SAY?
Have I convinced you yet that being in nature can be good for your health? I hope so! Here are a few Scriptures that

confirm we were meant to be a part of nature and we can even find God to a deeper level in the great outdoors.

God spoke: "Let us make human beings in our image, make them reflecting our nature so they can be responsible for the fish in the sea, the birds in the air, the cattle, and, yes, Earth itself, and every animal that moves on the face of Earth." God created human beings; he created them godlike, reflecting God's nature. He created them male and female. God blessed them: "Prosper! Reproduce! Fill Earth! Take charge! Be responsible for fish in the sea and birds in the air, for every living thing that moves on the face of Earth." Genesis 1:26 (The Message)

For since the creation of the world God's invisible qualities – his eternal power and divine nature – have been clearly seen, being understood from what has been made, so that men are without excuse. Romans 1:20 (NIV)

The LORD is my shepherd; I shall not be in want. He makes me lie down in green pastures, he leads me beside quiet waters, he restores my soul. Psalm 23:1-3a (NIV)

THE 30/30 EXPERIENCE

I remember the first time I saw snow. I was a young teenager and as we drove up the curvy mountain road leading to a winter retreat I saw it first alongside the road. My expectations grew! When we finally pulled over for a rest stop, I was out of the car before the parking brake set. I found a huge pile of snow in a nearby field and ran to fling myself, head-first, into that fluffy white powder. I do wish someone had warned me that not all piles are soft snow...some are rocks covered with snow! I survived the head injury but have never forgotten the wonder of my first snow.

We all need that wonder, those moments of reflection in nature, time to clear our head (not bang it!) by walking along a wooded path or sitting by the ocean listening to the waves crash on the shore. Studies indicate being in nature is an essential component of holistic health; and God encourages, or maybe even requires it as part of our spiritual well-being.

So what is the solution to Nature Deficit Disorder? What challenge can be presented here to help us overcome anxious moments and calm our spirits? It's simple enough really. Go outside. I know, I could have just said that at the beginning of the chapter and left it at that! However, perhaps you needed to be convinced first that it is necessary. How do I make being out in nature a regular part of my life?

> *"The sky's awake, so I'm awake, so we have to play."* Anna to Elsa in Frozen

The 30/30 Experience! Merriam-Webster defines a habit as a tendency or usual manner of behavior. It is also something that, done over time, becomes nearly or completely involuntary. In the 30/30 experience you will have the opportunity to develop the habit of enjoying nature as a way to reflect, relax, and respond to God's promptings in your life.

The goal of the 30/30 Experience is to spend 30 minutes outside in the next 30-40 days. As Richard Louv states, *"To take nature and natural play away from children may be tantamount to withholding oxygen."*[44] Could this also be true of adults?

Plan to be outside for 30 minutes every day. You can be energetic by going for a walk or a bike ride. You can play games like disc golf or corn-hole. Invite a friend for coffee and sit on the porch to drink it. You can be more reflective by sitting under a tree and praying, or getting lost in a good book. The options are endless for what to do on your 30/30.

I created the 30/30 experience for a class I was teaching and have done many of these when I find life is becoming overwhelming. They have been life changing! If you are like me you should feel better in your mind, body, and soul. Hopefully you'll develop the habit of making sure being in God's creation is a regular part of your healthy-living lifestyle.

THE CHALLENGE
Consider starting a 30/30 Experience as soon as possible. Get in God's creation, relax and breathe! What have you got to lose? Go for it!

TO THINK ABOUT...
1. How is my time in nature (outside)?

2. Do I believe this could help my life calm down some? How?

3. Can I do a 30/30 experience? When should I start?

Chapter 10

YOU ARE WHAT YOU EAT

Creating a Balanced Diet

By Laura Hall

As a Registered Dietitian Nutritionist (RDN), friends and acquaintances will ask me a bunch of questions about nutrition. "How do I lose weight?" "What about the [fill in the blank] diet?" "What is the one thing I should be eating?" My answer is there is not one thing that people should be doing or eating or not eating. In fact, a healthy lifestyle includes a *variety* of foods, *balanced* together with treats in *moderation*.

Billions of dollars are spent on weight loss products and books every year.[45] People will look for a quick fix and turn to fad diets. These fad diets tend to leave out food groups (no carbs for example), make false claims, and use partial science to explain weight loss or they will try to sell an expensive product. In fact, the word "diet" implies something that you start and then eventually end. A diet may work short term but people tend to gain the weight back and then some. The reality is fad diets do not produce lasting results. Instead, we need to think long-term, over a lifetime, and make dietary changes that will last. We need to consider ways to create a healthy lifestyle that will yield more benefits than just being on a diet.

REALISTIC GOALS AND BEHAVIOR CHANGE

Half of all American adults have one or more diet-related chronic diseases that are preventable, such as overweight/obesity, cardiovascular disease or type 2 diabetes.[46] Healthy changes are needed!

If someone wants to lose weight, first they need realistic goals, perhaps starting with a five pound weight loss. Cutting calories *too* low, tricks your body into thinking that it's starving and your metabolism will slow down. This is exactly the opposite of what you want happening when you're trying to lose weight! Instead,

> *The first thing you need to lose weight is a realistic goal.*

you want to lose weight gradually (1-2 pounds a week). For most people this means cutting out roughly 500 calories a day (from a combination of diet and exercise). Slower weight loss is more likely to be maintained long-term. So how do we do this? It takes a lifestyle change and a strong commitment to back it up.

The first step is to focus on positive eating and exercise behaviors and change unwanted negative behaviors. Pick one or two changes that are manageable and start there. If you make too many changes at once, you could decrease your chance of success. Incorporate just one change into your daily life until it becomes routine and then select another behavior to work on. For example, if you don't like vegetables it may be unrealistic to eat them at every meal but once you slowly add them into your diet, you might just find that you like them. Your body might actually crave them. I challenged several of my friends with this theory. They accepted the challenge and have been devouring vegetables ever since!

FOCUS ON VARIETY, BALANCE & MODERATION

The Dietary Guidelines for Americans encourage healthy eating patterns across the lifespan so that individuals stay within the calories *their* body needs to maintain a healthy weight and reduce their risk of chronic disease. Choosing a *variety* of nutrient-dense foods will help you meet all of your vitamin and mineral needs. What are nutrient-dense foods? Milk is a good source of calcium and vitamin D. Oranges are a good source of vitamin C. Salmon is a good source vitamin D and omega-3's. Another great example is bell peppers. They have vitamin K, A, E, folate, and potassium. As a general rule of thumb, the darker the color, the more nutrient-dense. Include as much "natural" color in your meals as you can. The nutrients you put into your body are important, *"Do you not know that your body is a temple of the Holy Spirit within you, whom you have from God? You are not your own, for you were bought with a price. So glorify God in your body."* (1 Corinthians 6:19-20 ESV)

On the other hand, *empty calories* provide calories and not much else (i.e. soda). In fact, these liquid calories, such as a fancy sugar-sweetened coffee, add up fast and we don't feel as satisfied from them. We need to limit calories from added sugars and saturated fat and decrease our sodium intake. The Dietary Guidelines recommend shifting to nutrient-dense foods/beverages across and within all food groups while considering cultural and personal preferences.

We need to *balance* our choices. If you choose a less nutrient-dense food for one meal like potato chips, make sure to include more nutrient-dense sources at the next meal such as a baked potato with salsa, corn and black beans. *Moderation* in our diets allows for treats or "fun food" as I tell my children. Once you have met your nutrient needs (iron, calcium, etc.) using nutrient-dense foods, you can include a "fun food" into your day without going over your total calories needed. How do we meet these nutrient needs? The government actually has some resources to help us put the dietary guidelines into practice.

CREATE A HEALTHY COLORFUL PLATE

The *Choose My Plate*[47] website gives us helpful tips on how to create a healthy colorful plate. The recommendation is to fill up half of your plate with fruits and veggies, ¼ should be grains, and another ¼ should include protein. They also emphasize approximately three servings of dairy (or calcium-fortified beverages) and healthy oils. On the website you can look up the specific number of servings for each food group at different calorie levels. For example if you need 2200 calories a day the chart will show how much fruit, vegetables, grains, and proteins you'll need to consume. They recommend choosing a variety of vegetables, such as dark greens, red and orange veggies and legumes (beans and peas).

Make sure to choose whole fruits and limit the intake of your fruit in the form of a juice. Vary your protein sources, such as seafood, lean meats, poultry, eggs, legumes, nuts, seeds and soy products. Make half of your grains whole grains, such as oatmeal, brown rice and whole grain bread/pasta. For calcium, choose fat-free or low-fat dairy or fortified beverages. Eat less food that is high in solid fat (butter/lard) and added sugars from all of the food groups.

Each food group is important to get a variety of nutrients but watch out for oversized portions. Make healthier choices at restaurants keeping these guidelines in mind. We tend to eat the same volume at meals so add veggies to meals and snacks because they are low in calories and high in fiber, which helps you feel full. Don't let these guidelines become so legalistic that you forget to enjoy your meals. When you can, be adventurous and try new foods!

GLORIFYING GOD

What is our motivation? Are we trying to look like a super model or professional athlete? Are our goals realistic? Perhaps, having the energy to chase after great-grandchildren in the distant future is a tangible goal to encourage us to eat healthy and exercise over a lifetime. You will need to decide your own healthy, tangible, and realistic goals.

At the end of the day, we need to love and appreciate and care for the *one body* God gave us. Scripture tells us we are *"fearfully and wonderfully made."* (Psalm 139:14

ESV) If you stop for a moment and really consider how God has designed our bodies to turn all that food into energy to run and jump and play, it is amazing! We need to take care of ourselves so that we live long healthy lives using our talents to glorify God. We are made in God's image (Genesis 1:27) and He created our bodies to come in different sizes and shapes. Even though we want the best *our body* can give us we also need to accept and embrace the diversity in our bodies. Having a positive body image is also an important part of a healthy lifestyle.

> We need to accept and embrace the diversity in our bodies.

Remember successful weight loss strategies include setting up reasonable goals, avoiding quick fixes, encouraging small changes, promoting positive behaviors, and including regular physical activity. Finding social support, addressing stress and getting adequate sleep are important too!

THE CHALLENGE

Explore the ChooseMyPlate website[48] and look up the number of servings that you need from each food group. Keeping all of the above in mind, try putting together a healthy plate and stay within your calories. Also check out the "What's Cooking? USDA Mixing Bowl" website.[49] It is an interactive website to help you with meal planning, grocery shopping, and cooking. You can look up recipes, save them into a cookbook, print recipe cards and even share them via social media. Your challenge for the week is to try a new recipe or two, eat better and have fun doing it! May God bless your journey and pursuit toward healthy eating.

TO THINK ABOUT...

1. What are my health and nutrition goals? *List a few that are realistic and reasonable:*

2. What are two positive behaviors I can work on?

3. How can I specifically add more vegetables and fruit to my meals so that they cover half of my plate?

4. What can I apply from this chapter as I plan a healthy meal, whether in a school cafeteria, a restaurant or my own home?

Chapter 11

CREATIVITY IS NOT A LUXURY

Exploring the Arts

By Emily Hill

"In the beginning God created…"[50] This is the first thing He tells us. So often we brush past these five words, eager to rush on to the heavens and earth forming, the light and dark separating. We read for the results of this passage. The water. The grass. The stars.

However, the Bible - the divinely inspired, holy, incorruptible word of the living God – starts with these first five words. And if we pause and ruminate on them, something profound emerges.

In the beginning, creativity was not an afterthought. It wasn't relegated to a childhood pastime, an afterschool hobby, an impractical major, a dead-end job. A secret unattainable wish, hidden under mountains of expectation, judgement, fear, and shame. Creativity wasn't a luxury. It was the beginning.

COLORING OUTSIDE THE LINES

Pause for a moment and think back to when you were a child. Do you remember singing a song at the top of your lungs? Mixing flavors of a soda to create something new? Playing dress up, pretending, imagining? Did you ever pick up a marker and press it to paper, just to see what would happen? These are the impulses of a people created to create.

They are the impulses God gave each and every one of us, not just the artists, musicians, and writers. He designed all humanity in His image. So as the professor explores ways of teaching, the chef pairs flavors in recipes, the analyst designs new systems…they are creating. Just as God intended.

For how can we as a people, made in the image of the God who created the universe, not create? To deny our creativity is to deny how God created us. Our creativity is a reflection of Him. He isn't concerned with our product or perfection. His primary focus, as always, is our

> *For how can we as a people, made in the image of the God who created the universe, not create?*

heart. Once upon a time when we were children, we knew this. We didn't worry about singing off key or looking silly or failing. We didn't fear coloring outside of the lines.

That fearlessness must be our goal again. We must take creativity off the shelf where it has been hidden away gathering dust. It is not luxury or indulgence. It is not a product or a result. Creativity is part of God's character – just like love, justice, mercy, and grace – and it is necessary to your physical, emotional, and spiritual health.

What if we stopped looking for results – for a product we deem worthy? What if, instead, we simply create for the love of it? For the sake of trying to be a little more like the God we serve?

THE RESULTS OF CREATIVITY

The results of creativity are staggering for physical and mental wellbeing. An extensive study on the health and wellbeing benefits of the arts and creativity found art therapies "alleviated anxiety and depression while increasing resilience and wellbeing" and after participating in art programs, "79% of people ate more healthily, 77% engaged in more physical activity, and 82% enjoyed greater well-being."[51] The very act of creating not only led to improvements to mental health but also produced healthier lifestyle choices in many of the participants. What an incredible testimony to the importance of creativity in our lives.

Sadly, while research shows benefits of creativity, it is still treated as luxury in many areas. Adobe's "State of Create" study found that "76% of Americans believe creativity is valuable to society, while 61% of Americans didn't feel they were living up to their creative potential."[52] A majority reported a lack of opportunities to be creative at work, in school, or in their spare time as a major contributor. This reinforces that we cannot wait for the world to offer space for creativity. We must learn to make intentional time in our lives to create.

"You can't use up creativity. The more you use the more you have."
Maya Angelou

Furthermore, a report from the World Economic Forum projects creativity will move from the 10th most important work skill in 2015, to the 3rd most important work skill by 2020.[53] This reveals creativity isn't just a necessity for our emotional and physical wellbeing. It is also necessary for our workplace success.

As always, it is amazing to see how scientific studies reflect the word of God. These statistics are profound, but simply illuminate what God has designed.

CREATED TO CREATE

In *Walking on Water*, Madeleine L'Engle explores the connection between art and faith. She specifically explores the creativity children have naturally. She says, "We write, we make music, we draw pictures, because we are listening for meaning, feeling for healing. And during the writing of the story or the painting or the composition or singing, we are returned to the open creativity which was ours when we were children."[54] The miraculous, undeniable creativity of the child reflects that human beings were created to create.

The Bible speaks repeatedly of humanity being made in God's image, as well as the unique giftings given to His children. One such example is in Exodus, during the creation of the Tabernacle. Moses speaks to the people, inspired by God's word to him, *"See, the LORD has called by name Bezalel the son of Uri, son of Hur, of the tribe of Judah; and He has filled him with the Spirit of God, with ability, with intelligence, with knowledge, and with all craftsmanship..."* (Exodus 35: 30-31 RSV)

What a beautiful example of God's intentionality in placing a special artistic call on one of his children. As Gene Veith explores in his book, *State of the Arts*, "Bezalel is the first person described in the scriptures as being filled with the Holy Spirit."[55] Yet again, God reveals His value of creative pursuits.

Nevertheless, perhaps you don't think creativity is one of your gifts. Genesis reveals God created all mankind in his image. *"So God created man in His own image, in the image of God he created him: male and female he created them."* (Genesis 1:27 NKJV) This early in Genesis, only a few traits of God have been shown. Many more traits will come to light through the rest of the Bible. But here, in the very first chapter, we learn God is creative. And He created us to be like Him. Surely then, creativity is a necessity for human beings.

Whether you have been given a particular gift of artistry, are still exploring the endless ways to create, or don't think you have a creative bone in your body, you are God's image bearer. You are creative. You have been created to create.

THE CHALLENGE: LET'S GET STARTED

I hope, by now, you want to create. Your fingers itching to paint, your lips pairing words together, your mind dreaming. But as with many things, we feel the pull, the tug, the call, but we don't know how to put one step in front of the other. How to take creativity off the shelf of luxury and make it a habit. As with many of the principles of wellbeing, it is a learned skill. One that takes time and practice. One you might forget about for a time, return to, and have to awaken.

Here are some practical steps to try today:

- Find a quiet space and listen to praise music. Focus on the lyrics and melody.
- Make a collage of your favorite pictures to keep on your desk or in a notebook.
- Get a coloring book. Color one picture each evening before bed.
- Try a new recipe for dinner or dessert once a week.
- Use paints and mix colors. Don't try to make anything. Just explore the vast array of colors.
- Create a new outfit with the clothes in your wardrobe.

As you begin, give yourself time to find your creativity again. It might take time. You might fear you don't know how. But you are a child of the God who created the universe, and everything in it. You are created in His image. His spirit lives inside you, empowering forgiveness, grace, and creativity. Remember this: *In the beginning God created.* And so must we.

TO THINK ABOUT...

1. In what ways was I creative as a child? Art, music, make believe, etc. Can I remember if or when I stopped doing those things?

2. What things keep me from being creative? Is it fear of failure? Lack of time or practice?

3. Have I ever experienced one of the benefits of creativity? Perhaps a solution at work that I solved through creativity, or a time when being creative helped my emotional well-being?

4. Consider the concept of being made in God's image. In what ways do I feel like I reflect the image of God? In what ways do I want to grow in this area?

Chapter 12

INTO THE DEEP END

Drowning in Technology and Social Media

By Matthew Bach

Progress and innovation have hurled you into a technologically advanced world. Most likely you own not only a smart phone and laptop, but smart watches, iPads, wireless headphones, game consoles, etc. You can engage with people 24-7 on numerous platforms and with a variety of mediums (pictures, videos, texts, etc.). Technology is present everywhere and encompasses a majority of our important relationships. An amusing commercial for ATT perfectly displays this as Mark Wahlberg explains that we want all our things to be television things, we want all our shows to go with us anywhere, we want everything *unlimited*. He finishes with: "food, water, *internet*...we *need* it to live."

Even though this has become a constant backdrop to your life, having a greater power than education, government, or church[56]; what happens when and if you feel like you're drowning in it? Or worse, what if you cannot sense yourself sinking slowly, but feel anxious, overwhelmed, purposeless and empty? We want to delineate how you can use technology and social media, so it does not use you.

THE POWER OF TECHNOLOGY & MEDIA

Gregory Jantz states, "*Everyday something is working hard to hook your attention, to compel your focus, to dominate your mind.*"[57] Even as I worked on this chapter, I spent numerous days wasting time on my devices engaging with various media. I would tell myself to turn it off, put it down and focus. But I struggled to listen to that inner voice and couldn't compel myself to quit. Sound familiar? We need to take notice of anything that works so mercilessly to take up so much time in life. It's much stronger than we realize, for its power concerns the very core need of our identity.

Its attraction lies in things you can personalize. It becomes your profile and presence - an extension of your identity.[58] It puts words and images to issues and situations you experience and so you reach out anxiously to embrace it. This is something formidable. It can draw us in psychologically and emotionally. It alters our world and expectations, reprograms us, and even defines who we are. J.R.R. Tolkien built this concern on the power of technology into his classic story, *The Lord of the Rings*. He writes to his editor that:

> Anyway, all this stuff is mainly concerned with Fall, Mortality, and the Machine...By the last I intend all use of external plans or devices *instead of* [the] development of the inherent inner powers or talents -- or even the use of these talents with the corrupted motive of dominating: bulldozing the real world, or coercing other wills.[59]

Tolkien saw something behind the powerful technology of his day and crafted his story of a community fighting to prevent its dominance or misuse. We, as a community, must look deeper beneath technology and social media. Because of the power technology holds it *must* be approached with caution. Yet, many of us abandon wisdom when it comes to the latest upgrade or the newest tech convenience or

> *The power technology holds must be approached with caution.*

the most palatable media fad.[60] In the end, I care about true wholeness for you and me. That we would not live in partial attention and partial distraction, but in vibrant encounter with one another and our Lord.

WHY FLOAT IN DISENCHANTMENT?

Because you have major access to the lives of others in real time, you able to engage with their stories and updates and also assess their world. This is where the tension lies, for when we assess someone's witticisms and exciting pictures, our default is not to celebrate with them, but feel worse about our life. For the competitive in heart, we're compelled to go and create a more exciting life and share it. There is an increased pressure to appear successful and happy, to be familiar with all things 'culture', and post or share every minute of it. If any of us are faltering in self-worth, it creates a level of disenchantment that pushes us under the water. We don't know what to do about it all. And we keep scrolling...

Our hearts don't need to be stifled, instead, we need to heed Proverbs 4:23, *"Above all else, guard your heart, for it is the wellspring of life."* In scripture, the heart[61] is not only the seat of our emotions, but also the locus of our thinking, remembering, choosing, and planning. In other words, the heart refers to the inner person in its various aspects. When we observe that the human heart is prominent in scripture, we see that the Lord is concerned first and foremost with our inner life. He is committed to the renovation of our hearts and desires us to live full and free. His Spirit creates community by which we can sustain the transformation He initiates by the sacrifice of Jesus on the cross. So why allow ourselves to float in such disenchantment?

CONDUCT LIFE WISELY
Let me direct your eyes to Colossians 4:5, *"Be wise in the way you act towards outsiders; make the most of every opportunity."*[62] (NKJV) As your moving through a digital world, conduct life wisely. Wisdom is handling life and all its challenges in a way that pleases God. Paul instructed the Colossians to be filled with wisdom (1:9-10) and that all the treasures of God's wisdom are found in Christ (2:3). So living wisely means living *centered on Jesus.* Paul uses a commercial term to add gravity to this command: *buy up/redeem the time* (making the most of). This concerns the quality of time, that these are "never to be repeated" opportunities for God to shine through you. So, as you swim among the torrents of technology and media, you can gauge and modify technology's grip in

your life, and learn, in God's wisdom, how to *use it* so it does not use you.

THE CHALLENGE

Invite Others to Check Your Usage.

Are we in a community of transformation? Does the way we engage with one another in real life and digital life, reflect a commitment to the transformation of our hearts? Since most media is viewed in private, very few people know about the content or quantity of our streaming, searching, posting or communication. The first step is to no longer allow this to remain secretive and individual. We want to be transparent, so that as a community we thrive and have personal accountability.

Try a Tech and Media Fast.

So many people share their difficulty in hearing or seeing God. Perhaps this is the inspiration to remove the distractions, and be free to focus on something else, such as the Lord. In those times when you feel bored or overwhelmed and slide into

> *Try a media fast for 24 hours!*

listening, watching, searching, or scrolling; allow God to be your fixation. You may realize how addictive all of this is without a proper outlet. Addiction is present when you find yourself anxious, antsy, extremely bored, or hangry (hungry + angry).[63] Start small and try fasting for 24 hours. See the effect it leaves on your spirit and sense of identity.

Look at it as Mission.

Warren Wiersbe describes ministry as "God's resources, meeting human needs, through loving channels, to the glory of God."[64] We may not realize that ministry can occur in online and digital settings, as much as in a life to life setting. We should recognize that if social media was a country, it would be the largest population in the world (like almost 2 billion people). How do we see opportunities to ask thought-provoking questions or share our faith in these spheres? To act as ambassadors who stand at the intersection between two countries, using our knowledge of both cultures to build a bridge of understanding between the two.

What if we could use social media to encourage others, to share what Christ is teaching us, or to make it about serving rather than receiving? I remember one summer joining some high school students each Thursday to do street witnessing, prayer walks and gospel discussions. One evening I had us spend time sitting at a Peet's Coffee, opening our Instagram, and choosing 10+ people to message with words of encouragement and blessing. Ninety minutes of pure digital outreach. Nearly every person we messaged replied with gratitude and enthusiasm, almost like they've never received such encouragement on this medium. There is power in these digital loving channels to participate in God's work.

TO THINK ABOUT...

1. Does anyone know what I watch/access or how much time I am on my devices? Have I invited anyone to ask me about my usage?

2. Are there friends or family I give permission to tell me when I am on tech too much; or whether my stress-busyness may be tied to technology?

3. Do I find myself agitated when I don't have access to tech and media? Am I addicted? How did I feel after trying a 24 hour fast?

4. Which media platforms can I use to serve others? *Try narrowing in on 10-20 people you have regular meaningful contact with and asking God what you can do to help them thrive.*

Chapter 13

NO TIME!

Practical Time Management

By Michael Obermire

Part 1 of 2

Laura was ten minutes late to her 7:50am Marketing class on that sunny September morning. If the already 79-degree temperature was any indication, it would be another hot day in northern California. As she entered the room to the notice of her teacher and friends, she thought to herself that being late wasn't her fault. No, she only overslept because she was studying late for the two quizzes her teachers had scheduled this week plus the presentation she had due as well. "Don't the faculty talk to each other?" she thought. Besides, her roommate in the small off campus apartment where she lived had finished the pot of coffee, so Laura had to buy a cup while putting gas in her car this morning. On top of everything, the front parking lot was being paved so she had to park at the back of the campus; the farthest spot from her morning class. This was no way to start the week.

Laura is right; already behind schedule at 8:00am Monday morning is a lousy way to start any week. However, is she correct that it is not her fault? Carl Pullein wrote[65],

Time is the most equal of equal opportunities employers. Every day, we all have exactly the same amount of time. Nobody has more or less. We have twenty-four hours. It does not matter whether you are Tim Cook, Warren Buffett or a freshman in college; we all face the same decisions every day about where to spend our time...It's no good blaming other people, your email or phone.

Laura needs to understand what part of time management is under her control, and what is not.

OWNING YOUR TIME

It is easy to understand why Laura might feel the way she does. From her perspective, the issues that interfered with her plans were uncontrollable events. How can she control the uncontrollable? What Laura is failing to grasp is that she had plenty of advanced notice on what was coming up, but didn't plan her time well enough to get the important things done. The key idea is "her time." She owns 24 hours of each day and it is up to her to assign the tasks for every hour. Yes Laura, you own *your* time; we all do.

Of course, parts of your day are effectively pre-assigned. Sleeping, eating, meeting personal needs are all necessities of life and will take up 8-12 hours every day. That still leaves 12-16 hours for work, school and fun: we will call this time your *uptime*. Planning how to prioritize activities during uptime is the key to getting everything (the fun stuff and work stuff) completed, on time and with limited stress. Managing uptime successfully will create balance and a feeling of accomplishment.

On the previous Wednesday Laura knew she had quizzes and a team project due the next week. So why was she so stressed?

"How did you do on the quiz?" asked Owen from her Marketing class. "Pretty easy, huh?"

"No, actually," replied Laura with a low voice and eyes cast downward. "I thought it was hard."

Laura walked alone to the Shack, the coffee shop on campus, to get a Latte and donut. That combination tended to make life better, at least momentarily, and she could study for her next quiz in 50 minutes. But first she would check emails and her Instagram account. Laura had posted some great pictures over the weekend.

In order to manage uptime, we must write down our daily plan or at least a to-do list. To understand what activities are important each day, we need to use a planning horizon of at least one week; two weeks would be even better. Use any method that works for you: a calendar, sticky notes, your phone notepad, paper and pencil, but get your plan on a document. Don't rely on your memory.

Start with obvious entries. In Laura's case it is due dates for tests, papers, homework and presentations. For you it might be work projects, lunches, getting an oil change on the car or a dental appointment. Next, add in a *specific plan* on when you will accomplish each one of your entries. Every assignment or project has different time requirements, so scheduling the time ahead is a big step closer to a great outcome.

The Bible has something to say about time management, recognizing the many areas of life that we need to accomplish in a given time.

There is a time for everything, and a season for every activity under the heavens:
a time to be born and a time to die,
> *a time to plant and a time to uproot,*
a time to kill and a time to heal,
> *a time to tear down and a time to build,*
a time to weep and a time to laugh,
> *a time to mourn and a time to dance,*
a time to scatter stones and a time to gather them,
> *a time to embrace and a time to refrain from embracing,*
a time to search and a time to give up,
> *a time to keep and a time to throw away,*
a time to tear and a time to mend,
> *a time to be silent and a time to speak,*
a time to love and a time to hate,
a time for war and a time for peace. (Eccl. 3:1-8 NIV)

FOCUS ON HIGH VALUE ACTIVITIES

One of the most difficult aspects of good time management is learning to

> *Learn to separate the "can and should be done", from the "must be done."*

separate the *can* and the *should be done*, from the *must be done!* For instance, Laura stopped to get gas on Monday morning before her early class. A better plan would have been to fill up over the weekend. Working (if you have a job), sleeping, eating and having gas in your car are in the "must be done" category. Completing assignments or work projects on time and being prepared for what you know will happen today are also in this category. Technology including the ever-present social media, watching Netflix, or playing video games can be major disrupters of anyone's day, but they are in the "can be done" category and should not trump activities that must be done. The editor of the Purdue University Blog gives this advice specifically to students,

It's easy to get distracted. Pay attention to what draws your focus away from your studies and assignments. Are you spending too much time checking social media? Are you prone to texting and answering personal phone calls while studying? Do you find that a lot of time has passed while you aimlessly browse the web? No matter what is wasting your time, set a goal to not engage in that behavior during dedicated study time. Instead, use those activities as a reward for staying focused and accomplishing the tasks you set out to complete.[66]

ASK FOR SUPPORT

In your attempts to practice good time management, you can recruit others to help. Support can come from parents, roommates, classmates, coworkers, pastors, teachers, and coaches. Assistance may look like working in study groups before exams, ride sharing to save money, or asking a friend for accountability on your to-do list. Even something as simple as keeping a household running grocery list can make shopping easier and faster. The Bible confirms the positive effect of teamwork, *"Two are better than one, because they have a good return for their labor: If either of them falls down, one can help the other up. But pity anyone who falls and has no one to help them up."* (Ecclesiastes 4:9-10 NIV)

REVIEW & REVISE

Lastly, review your plan at the end of each day and revise when necessary. Reschedule those items that you didn't accomplish today into a future day. Sometimes this may entail reworking multiple days to fit in everything. Don't beat yourself up because today didn't go as planned. They rarely do. The key is to have a workable plan that is achievable. Nothing breeds success like success.

Two weeks later Laura was speaking to her dad on the phone.

"Hi honey," said a very happy father. "It's good to hear you voice."

"Jeez dad, we talk every week," explained Laura.

"Still, can't a dad like to talk to his daughter? So was last week easier since you started your time management routine?" inquired dad.

"Yes it was. This planning stuff actually works. Thanks for your help," answered a very sincere daughter.

Dad's next question was on a more serious note. "Since you have less than three semesters left before graduation, have you thought about personal goals?"

Laura was quick with her response, "My only goal is to survive this semester."

"We will talk more when you come home this weekend. Goal setting is fun stuff. We can talk over dinner. I'm smoking a salmon Saturday." Dad knew it was Laura's favorite meal.

THE CHALLENGE

Try it! Make a two-week plan identifying the key activities that you need to accomplish giving yourself sufficient time to complete each one. Focus on separating the could-be done from the must-be done activities. Work hard for two weeks consistently reviewing and revising your plan every night and watch your time management improve!

TO THINK ABOUT...

1. Am I spending too much time on social media? Should I begin to keep track of this on an app?

2. How would a thoughtfully prepared plan help me specifically organize my time?

3. What do I need to do first? When can I start a two-week trial period of practicing good time management?

Chapter 14

Moving Forward

Successful Goal Setting

By Michael Obermire

Part 2 of 2

After they had finished eating the Salmon dinner and cleaning up, Laura sat down with her father in the living room.

"I am proud of the progress that you have made in managing your schoolwork, spiritual time, work, and fun time. You seem happier, more rested, and your grades are really good," started Laura's father, Jim. "Since you will be graduating in just three more semesters, it's time to establish some goals, don't you think?"

"So surviving isn't a good enough goal," asked Laura?

"No honey, surviving is expected; thriving is hoped for, but a goal must be deeper, and more personal," explained Jim. "Goals help define where you are headed today, next week and next year. Perhaps after the exodus from Egypt if the Israelites had a well-defined goal of pleasing God they wouldn't have been lost for 40 years." Jim was speculating now but trying to make a good point.

"OK Dad I get it. Let me think on it and we can talk again next week. Would that be OK with you," asked Laura?

"That will be fine honey."

C.S. Lewis said, "You are never too old to set a new goal or dream a new dream."[67] I might add that we are never too young either. Dreams and goals are a vessel on the same path; the difference is that a dream becomes a goal when you add when and how you will accomplish it. Many books and articles have been written about how to approach creating personal goals. The American Intercontinental University suggests the S.M.A.R.T. approach.

S.M.A.R.T.

Specific – Know exactly what you need to accomplish and what you hope to gain from doing so, whether it's simply finishing a paper or project, or something larger.

Measurable – Make sure you can easily evaluate whether or not your goal was met and how beneficial it ultimately was to you.

Achievable – Be realistic when setting goals. This can help you avoid missing deadlines and getting behind, as well as giving you a more accurate overview of how much time you have to invest in other tasks throughout the week.

Results-Focused – Have very clear, distinct outcomes for meeting your goals, and hold yourself to them.

Time-Bound – Set a deadline for each goal or, for more complex tasks with multiple steps, establish deadlines for each major stage of the process.[68]

The same process should be used when approaching larger goals such as career choices, graduate degree programs, and home ownership. It is impossible to understand the progress you've made with a goal unless you measure where and when you began, and compare it to where you are now. Realistically you are not going to cure world hunger next month, but you could volunteer at a shelter and help feed those in need. Great journeys begin with a single step.

> *If you aim for nothing, you'll hit it every time.*
> Source Unknown

Laura was having trouble getting started in her goal setting process. She couldn't think of any goals important enough to write down, so she asked her friends for help over lunch.

"My Dad wants me to write down some goals, now that I manage my time so well." (groans from her friends), "And I'm stuck. Any ideas? Do you guys have goals?" asked Laura.

"Like what? Straight A's or something?" inquired Tammy.

Julie thought she understood. "I had to set up personal goals for an assignment in my Communications class. It wasn't too hard. One was about getting more sleep, one was getting an A in my Management class, and the best was reducing my personal best time in the mile by 15 seconds."

Laura asked, "So even little stuff can become a goal? Not that shaving 15 seconds off your mile time is little."

"Yep," said Julie, "all kinds of big and small stuff can become a goal. The key is the other parts of goals, like a time to complete and how to measure. Adding that stuff makes it a goal."

The lunch friends agreed to meet the next day in Laura's apartment to help her find the right goals.

Even Jesus set goals, as shown in Luke. *"At that time some Pharisees came to Jesus and said to him, 'Leave this place and go somewhere else. Herod wants to kill you.' He replied, 'Go tell that fox, 'I will keep on driving out demons and healing people today and tomorrow, and on the third day I will reach my goal.'"*[69]

Jesus set a specific time when He would reach His goal, and what He would do (driving out demons and healing people today and tomorrow) until He was ready. Achieving a goal takes preparation, planning, and the ability to manage how you spend your time.

GOALS AND PYRAMIDS

Pyramids have a solid base, and each of the sides rises to the top where they all meet at the apex, the highest point of a pyramid. Imagine that your goal resides at the top of the pyramid. To climb to the top and reach your goal, first all the work of creating the base and building the walls, one brick at a time, must be completed.

> At the bottom of the pyramid you'll find hard work, sacrifice, prayers, and support.

At the bottom of the pyramid you'll find hard work, sacrifice, prayers, and support. For a college student that may include excellent homework turned in on time, long workouts in the gym, and late nights at a job. Your list might be comprised of paying attention to details, diligent work hours and turning in reports to supervisors.

Further up from the bottom are plans, to do lists, and boxes checked as complete. In this section hard work is combined with clever ideas, weekly planners, specific ideas and measurements. With tenacity and prayer, the apex is now visible and the goal is reached. Cherish the moment, but not for too long. Now is the time to reach for the next goal, the next peak, another horizon.

Laura's meeting with her friends was productive and fun. She now had established some goals and written them into her notebook, along with a timeline for completion, and resources needed to meet each goal. One goal was straightforward – she was determined to earn an A in Macroeconomics, so she included extra time each week in her planner to study and complete projects. Laura also set a goal to join a club on campus this semester and eventually become an officer – she knew the value of an extracurricular activity on her resume. Finally, by the end of this semester, Laura will decide the industry she wants to work in so she can begin doing research and find an internship for next year. Her Dad will be happy.

SETBACKS AND FRUSTRATIONS

The letter to the Hebrews reminds us how to ask for help. *"Let us then approach God's throne of grace with confidence, so that we may receive mercy and find grace to help us in our time of need."* (4:16 NIV) We need God's help along the path of reaching goals, because embedded in the process are setbacks, frustration, and thoughts of giving up. It happens to everyone. Sometimes we must make adjustments in the timeline to accomplish a goal. Other times, we may need to add more resources or just work harder. Occasionally, we will simply fail at reaching a goal. Failure is a key ingredient to success.

Stephen Curry, arguably one of the greatest NBA players of all time, missed a 2-point shot 52.8% of the time during the 2018-19 regular season.[70] He made a lot of shots, but he also failed to make the shot more often than he made one. Yet, very few among us would ever say Stephen Curry is a failure in the NBA.

J.K. Rowling, an amazing author, has a thought on the height of a goal and failure. "Some failure in life is inevitable. It is impossible to live without failing at something, unless you live so cautiously that you might as well not have lived at all -- in which case, you fail by default."[71] Accept and learn from your failures as much as your successes.

THE CHALLENGE

Create three goals to accomplish during the next six months. Identify the time requirements and resources needed for each, and then do it!

TO THINK ABOUT...

1. What are some of my major accomplishments in life so far (write these down)? No matter where I am in life, I might be amazed at the things I have already accomplished!

2. What are some of my current goals? Do I have a specific and measureable way to reach them?

3. Is there a goal I want to accomplish in the next five years? Think big.

4. Do I have a dream that I can turn into a goal? Dream very big.

Chapter 15

THE POWER OF SAYING "NO"

Making Yes a Matter of Priorities

By Dave Heitman

It takes a lot of faith to say no. Decision-making causes anxiety in the best of us. Especially when saying no means forfeiting the infinite possibilities of what *could be* for the risk of what *might* be. Most people want to keep their options open and therefore say yes by default. Couple this with false Christian notions of not wanting to offend and we can suffer from the impossible "yes always" mindset.

What if saying yes to everything actually means we're indirectly saying no? What if God calls us to say no to lesser things so we can say yes to greater things? What if saying no actually fosters healthy boundaries and helps shape our identity in Christ? Freedom and wholeness can be found in the power of saying no. When Jesus said, *"Let your yes be yes and your no be no,"* he meant for no to be included in our vocabulary (Matthew 5:37).

On the surface, I'm the least qualified to write a chapter on saying no. My wife laughed when I told her I was writing this chapter, because I love to say yes – yes to God, yes to adventure, yes to helping a friend write a book. All these are "good yes's." However, I know something you know too: *none* of us can do it all. All of us have different capacities but everyone has limits. Life's limits are actually God's hidden blessings because they bring us to important decision points. I must confess, as a husband, father of four, a dean, and doctoral student, I smile inside when undergrads tell me how busy they are - not because I don't believe them, but because I do. And I know there's only more ahead. No matter what stage of life you are in, *now* is the perfect time to learn how to say yes and no to the right things.

THE "YES ONLY" FALLACY

Saying yes to God will never wear us out and, fortunately, never wears God out either. However, saying yes to other things can wear us out if we're not careful. That's why Jesus invites everyone to come to Him *"all who are burdened and heavy laden and I will give you rest."* (Matthew 11:28 NIV) I used to think great leaders and truly spiritual people said yes to everything. After crashing and burning enough times I know this isn't true. Saying yes isn't wrong. However, there are some notable unhealthy reasons for saying yes. An insincere yes to look better than we are, a prideful yes pretending to benefit others, a fearful or insecure yes, a convenient yes - when no is the correct answer. All of these are wrong reasons to say yes.

It is surprising but the first message Jesus preached began with a no. *"Repent for the kingdom of heaven is at hand;"* (Matthew 3:2 NIV). Essentially stop, turn, say no to your kingdom, and yes to my greater kingdom that is at hand. Early on Jesus went missing and the disciples looked for Him because many clamored for healing. But Jesus was away praying. With His popularity soaring,

Jesus said no, *"They searched for Jesus, and found him saying, 'Everyone is looking for you.' And he said, 'Let us go on to the next towns, that I may preach there also, for that is why I came.'"* (Mark 1:35-38 ESV) The disciples noticed Jesus' prayer time provided God's divine yes and no.

It's an interesting fact that the only time the disciples ever asked Jesus to teach them anything it was about how to pray. I would have asked Jesus about miracles, multiplying that kid's lunch, walking on water and the like. However, Jesus teaches the disciples to pray saying, *"Father, holy is your name. Your kingdom come..."* (Luke 11:1-4 NIV) Funny how in most of my prayers I only really want God to say, "Yes" to something for me.

SAYING NO TO SAY YES
Saying no to say yes is a matter of priorities. No one can do everything. If you plot your life on a pie graph there are only so many ways to slice your life and still make a whole you. Slicing a pie can only be done so many times before there are no slices left. There is a big difference between slicing pie and mashing potatoes. Saying yes to everything is like taking a pair of electric beaters to a freshly baked pie. Mashed pie anyone? My pastor used to say, "24 hours is always enough time to do God's will." If God wanted us to do more, He would have given more hours in the day. Saying yes may inadvertently mean saying no elsewhere in our lives if we're not careful.

Instead, we must understand saying no is hard but *not* saying no is even harder. While this generation is the most connected in history, statistics show we have never felt more isolated, anxious, and depressed. Statistics show we are more depressed than those who survived the Great Depression. That's depressing.

Saying no to lesser things like constant social media and screen time can literally make us happier. Our collective experience speaks to this. When the average student is asked how they are doing the common reply is "busy." Personally, I think busy is a dirty four letter word. Busy denotes we are slaves to our own lives. If I am busy, I probably said yes one too many times and it might benefit me and those around me to say no more often. For example, my family feels it the most when I am busy. We have to start saying no to lesser things in order to say yes to God and the important people he has placed in our lives.

> *Busy denotes we are slaves to our own lives. If I am busy, I probably said 'yes' one too many times.*

SAYING YES TO SAYING NO

Personal choice is both a privilege and a big responsibility. We all make choices and those choices ultimately make us. Others may provide wise counsel but ultimately *we alone make the choice.* We can't expect others to live the consequences for us because we allowed them to make our choice. I recommend making your own mistakes rather than using your life to make the mistakes of others. God gave us the opportunity to live out our own lives, to make choices, to say yes, and to say no.

Saying no is a gift. Saying no establishes boundaries and protects our yes from being robbed. During our wedding, my wife and I both agreed to say yes to saying no. While we said "I do's" to one another we were simultaneously saying no to everyone else in the world.

What I didn't realize was that "everyone else" included myself. Before, I knew I could be selfish but it wasn't until marriage that I learned how truly selfish I am. I still remember returning home from surfing past 9pm one summer night during our first month of marriage and finding my lovely wife sitting by herself at our little dining room table with a cold dinner in front of her. She wasn't saying I couldn't go surfing, she married a surfer. But she clearly communicated that she didn't marry me to eat alone. I'm slow but I quickly grasped marriage meant saying no to certain things to say yes to greater things. You will never regret saying no to lesser things in order to say yes to something or someone greater.

Ultimately we alone make the choice to say yes or no.

The Gospel is essentially a story of saying yes and no. God designed us to say yes to Him but gave us the choice to do so. Choosing someone else above all others is the key to intimacy. Unfortunately, our first parents, Adam and Eve, said yes to themselves and no to God and humanity has been making the same destructive choice ever since. However, God sent Jesus Christ as his eternal yes to the world by way of the cross. The high priest spoke truly when he mocked Jesus on the cross saying,

"He saved others; he cannot save himself." (Matthew 27:42 NIV) Jesus had the power to save Himself but said no in order to save us. His no to self was our forever yes toward God. Jesus said yes to saying no and saved the entire world!

CHALLENGE

Begin now to look at your life, your busy and hectic schedule and ask yourself, "Do I need to learn to say NO more often?" Look at your priorities. Are you able to do your very best in those areas? If not, are there areas that are suffering because you refuse to say no? If you do not get a handle on this it will affect you more than you can possibly imagine, so be diligent to make the necessary corrections in your life now.

TO THINK ABOUT...

1. Who gets the ultimate yes in my life: God or me? *Remember you cannot have it both ways.*

2. Do I say YES too often? If so, why do I think I do this?

3. Do I set my own priorities or does it seem that others set them for me?

4. What are those distractions that may keep me from saying *yes* to the right things?

5. What is one thing from this chapter that I need to remember when it comes to saying no?

Chapter 16

BOATS & BEST INTENTIONS

Career & Life Planning

By Christy Jewell

I can't recall my age exactly...maybe I was 13 years old. However, I can remember the setting, the time of year and my father's words. Growing up, I thought I wanted to be many things, from ballerina to teacher to a modern day Annie Oakley. What I did know about myself at that young age, was that I valued the outdoors, nature, animals and their care, justice, fairness and independence. I had read a book called *Frosty: A Raccoon to Remember*[72] and I immediately saw myself in the future: a forest ranger who adopts a young raccoon, and in her work, embodied all that I valued.

My father, who seemed to have that 6th 'love language'[73] that only a daughter of a fireman could understand, said, "A forest ranger? Why would you want to do that? You'll end up in Blythe cleaning pit toilets for a living!" Young and impressionable, and wanting to please my father and not disappoint, I walked away from that encounter feeling at a loss for what I could do with my life.

I tell this story a lot. I tell it to parents who don't realize how impactful their influence and words are to their children, who are trying to figure out what they want to do, and who they want to be. I tell it to students, who I encourage to connect with a professional mentor and do job shadowing in order to learn more about potential careers.

We spend a lot of time, especially in Christian higher education, talking about the idea of 'calling,' as we are surrounded with young adults moving through a transformational season in their lives. There are many definitions, opinions, and suggestions on how to 'find' one's calling, and as a byproduct of finding it, what we might do for our vocation or career. This assumed connection between calling and career has many people confused and frustrated by the misalignment of what they are doing (or not doing) in their lives for work. There is a collective Calling (capital C) for all believers to fulfill the Great Commission (Matthew 28:16–20). However, each believer has a different calling (small c) and role to play in this.

In his book *Leading from the Inside Out*, the author identifies key clues[74] one can use to determine their calling or career focus:

- Previous experiences
- Present circumstances
- Possible opportunities
- Personal gifts
- Prompting of the Holy Spirit
- Personal passions
- Private counsel

For those of us with a considerable number of candles on our birthday cakes, we know that each of these clues are things we build over time, and with age comes our ability to discern and gain wisdom from the clues. However, for a young person the strongest 'clues' or influences come from the trusted adults in their lives. My father's best intentions, which came from a place of true concern for my well-being and happiness, was nonetheless counsel that came from a place of ignorance. This is why I am so passionate about helping others find their way to engaging careers. Career planning is about helping people collect all of their 'clues' from a wide variety of places to help them begin to *trust moving forward* in their path to discover their calling through career.

Young people are often allowed to move through educational systems and their personal lives without any opportunities to experience hard-earned success, true failure, pride, shame, self-determination, conflict, loss or life-impacting moments where they can begin to define their values, gifts, passions and strengths.

Many of us may have even been fed the myth that if we listen hard enough and wait long enough, we will hear God's clear voice, His 'call' on our life. We may find ourselves paralyzed, somehow afraid to move anywhere either from FOMO (fear of missing out) or a lack of self-knowledge and resilience.

This is where I talk about BOATS. Boats are generally useless vessels unless they are doing one thing: *moving*. Only when put in motion are you able to steer it right, left, or even reverse. Only when accelerating can you discover and see things, experience new settings and correct for conditions that arise. Idle and waiting, a boat is at the whim of the waves and wind to determine where it will end up. You cannot steer an idle boat.

ENGAGING THE PROCESS

The process of career and life planning is not a one-and-done activity. It is ever changing, growing and adjusting due to a wide variety of circumstances. The career development process happens throughout our lives. We already know that we want to be a useful boat, one that is moving forward. However, how can we know the steps necessary to ensure we reach our destination, or at least enjoy the ride? How do we know that our boat is water-ready? The following steps will help us get "ship-shape"!

Step 1: KNOW YOURSELF *(IMAGINE)*
While in college, by identifying your interests, personality, and skills, you can choose a major that 'fits' you well. Keeping in mind that many majors are not a linear or direct connection to a vocational outcome, you can choose your coursework and major based on results you obtain from reliable career assessments. We encourage students to take the Clifton Strengths assessment[75] to identify their top five talent themes. Clifton Strengths are a great way to see how a complex Creator uniquely creates each of us. Scripture confirms this truth, *"I praise you because I am fearfully and wonderfully make; your works are wonderful, I know that full well."* (Psalm 139:14 NIV)

Step 2: EXPLORE OPTIONS *(INVESTIGATE)*

I try not to imagine how my life would have turned out differently if my dad had said, "Well I don't know what it takes to be a forest ranger or if you would like it, but I suggest you find someone who does and talk to them." Finding a professional mentor, engaging in informational interviewing and career exploration either online or face-to-face is priceless in its ability to guide and connect you with a career that aligns with your interests, values, and personality. This might save you a lot of time and heartache, as often learning more about an industry or career area is the best way to eliminate some things you may have not really understood were part of the job.

Step 3: GAIN CAREER EXPERIENCES *(INTERACT)*

Although a solid GPA and the reputation of your college may still hold some importance, employers value so much more than what happens in the classroom. Internships, employment while in college, volunteer experience, and extracurricular activities all rise to

> *Employers value so much more than what happens in the classroom.*

the top in what employers what from recent graduates.

Through these experiences, you will develop the necessary 'soft' skills or professional competencies, as well as the chance to build your professional network. Graduating with a college degree does not equal or entitle you to a professional entry-level job. Rather, it is the *degree alongside the experience* that makes you competitive.

Step 4: NETWORK, APPLY & PREPARE FOR TRANSITION *(IMPLEMENT)*

If you were diligent in Steps 1-3, this fourth step is a lot less daunting. Creating a winning résumé, cover letter, and LinkedIn profile are relatively easy tasks when you know yourself, your skills, experiences, and direction. The process of applying for work in our digital age can be a frustrating one, which is why the value of a professional network is essential. If more than 85 percent of jobs are found through a trusted network (not posted on a website) then maximizing those early experiences is essential to landing a great opportunity.

Finally, don't assume your first job is *the* job. If you want to get into an organization or industry, don't wait to be offered the perfect job there! Accept an entry-level position, even one outside your career area, and you will find your way around and UP once you are in. Most companies prefer to promote from within before going outside to fill their mid- and upper-management positions. When they see and know the value of you and your work, promoting to find the right fit at the right time will be much easier.

Do not put all your expectations for living out your calling and engaging all your values, interests, and spiritual gifts into your career. That gives a career too much responsibility and power of its own. You should like your occupation and have the opportunity to live in your Strengths in most areas of your work, but your job cannot meet all your expectations.

As I shared earlier, my values are being in nature, animals and their care, justice, fairness and independence. I get to live in my Strengths every day at work. I get to connect amazing students and alumni with people and opportunities in the region where I work; and do so independently. I am married to law enforcement (justice). I am an urban rancher, with 22 animal souls living on my one-acre in-town property. Am I living my calling? You bet I am.

THE CHALLENGE

Choose at least one of the following to begin to do now; find a career assessment to take, meet with a potential career mentor, engage in volunteer opportunities, and/or create and update your résumé.

TO THINK ABOUT

1. How can the ideas in this chapter help me move forward with confidence that with faithful work on my part, God will provide ways to reveal His plans for me?

2. What are my Strengths? How do I see myself using them in my future career?

3. What are my key values and interests as they pertain to calling or career?

4. Is my 'boat' moving forward? What do I need to do first to get some acceleration?

Chapter 17

BETTER BANK ACCOUNTS

Healthy Financial Habits

By Steve Backers

When we think about health, most people just think about physical health, but a more holistic view should also include mental health, spiritual health, *and financial health.* It is important to understand why we make the financial decisions we do, how it affects us, and why money plays such an integral role in our lives. Money is simply a tool to make an exchange; a method of payment. However, how we make decisions about the allocation of our financial resources tends to reflect what we value. According to Jim Taylor, "Your values form the foundation of your life. They dictate the choices you make and determine the direction that your life takes. Your values will influence your decisions related to your relationships, career, and other activities you engage in. Despite this importance, few people choose their values. Instead, they simply adopt the values of their parents and the dominant values of society."[76]

FINANCIALLY INDUCED STRESS

Do big financial decisions stress you out? Whenever we make big decisions about scarce resources like time and money, it generally induces stress and anxiety. According to Emmie Martin, "Americans are increasingly anxious about money. New data found that money is the number one cause of stress among Americans, according to 44 percent of survey respondents. Money is more of a problem than either personal relationships (25 percent) or work (18 percent)."[77]

While it may not be surprising that many of us experience financial stress, what might surprise you is that it's not relegated to those who don't have a lot of money. Some of the happiest people on earth have a lower standard of living and fewer resources than those in countries that are more affluent. "The World Database of Happiness, which measures the levels of happiness found in various nations according to a certain set of standards, often finds countries such as Costa Rica, Puerto Rico, and Mexico ranking above more affluent countries."[78]

Despite the abundance of research that money and possessions do not bring happiness, Americans continue to spend at record rates. In fact, Americans have purchased so much "stuff" that we have created a $38 billion personal storage industry to store our excesses![79]

> God created everything, we are merely stewards of what he gives to us.

Did you know money is one of the most covered topics in the Bible? It starts with the concept of stewardship, which is "the responsible overseeing and protection of something considered worth caring for and preserving."[80] The Bible teaches that God created everything and therefore it all belongs to Him. We are merely stewards of what He created and given to us. If we think of our money and other assets as His, we will spend it more wisely and give of it more generously. *"Now, our God, we give you thanks, and praise your glorious name. But who am I, and who are my people, that we should be able to give as generously as this? Everything comes from you, and we have given you only what comes from your hand."* (1 Chronicles 29:13-14 NIV) Here are four biblical habits for financial health to consider.

HABIT ONE: SPEND LESS THAN YOU EARN

Most people prefer instant gratification to delayed gratification. At the heart of instant gratification is what psychologists refer to as the pleasure principle, our innate desire to seek pleasure and avoid pain. This is why many of us don't have spending discipline. New technologies further enable our desire for immediate gratification. We can now order something and have it delivered two hours later thanks to Amazon Prime Now. Food delivery is no longer relegated to the neighborhood pizza joint. We can order dinner from a multitude of restaurants and have Uber Eats or Door Dash deliver it within 45 minutes! It's so easy and since it's all paid for electronically we really don't even feel the pain of paying for it. According to research from FINRA Investor Education Foundation's *Financial Capability in the United States 2016* report, about 60 percent of Americans spend all or more than their income.[81]

Action Step – Start tracking exactly where you money is going. Use an app like YNAB, Mvelopes, or Mint to make it easy and even link to your debit or credit card.

Try it for a day, then a week, then a month, until it becomes habit. Once you know your spending data, create a realistic budget and try to stick to it. Build a margin into your budget for the unexpected expenses.

HABIT TWO: AVOID DEBT

Avoiding debt is easier said than done for most of us. According to a Motley Fool 2017 article, "The average American household carries $137,063 in debt. Yet the U.S. Census Bureau reports that the median household income was just $59,039 last year, suggesting that many Americans are living beyond their means." [82]

Many students carry an additional burden when it comes to debt. Zack Friedman notes that, "Student loan debt is now the second highest consumer debt category — behind only mortgage debt — and higher than both credit cards and auto loans. Borrowers in the Class of 2017, on average, owed $28,650, according to the Institute for College Access and Success." [83]

The Bible doesn't say debt is a sin, but it does warn against debt. In pure financial terms, the only debt that makes sense is debt which generates greater financial return than its cost. Using a credit card you can't pay in full, doesn't generate a positive financial return. On the other hand, a home mortgage or a student loan may potentially deliver greater economic value than the cost of the debt. Real estate historically appreciates, and a college degree may lead to greater wage earning potential. In all cases, be cautious with debt and if you do use it, repay it as you promised.

Action Step – Only use a credit card if you are disciplined about paying the balance in full every month, otherwise you will likely be paying astronomical interest rates and digging an even deeper hole of debt. That said, having and using a credit card can help you build credit if you are able to pay the balance in full every month, but if you have any doubt in your ability to do that, use a debit card or automatic funds transfer so the money comes straight out of your account.

HABIT THREE: SAVE

Consistent with the personal spending and debt trends in America, savings rates are not great either. "Just 38 percent of Americans said they could cover an unexpected emergency room visit or even a $500 car repair with cash on hand in a checking or savings account, according to Bankrate."[84] "Twenty-nine percent of households have less than $1,000 in savings."[85]

Once you develop the saving habit, you will have the power of compounding on your side. If you're able to save just $100 a month, earning five percent per year, in ten years you will have put away $12,000, but it will have grown to over $15,000! *"The plans of the diligent lead to profit as surely as haste leads to poverty."* (Proverbs 21:5 NIV)

Action Step – Start with a small amount, relative to your income, but set up an automatic savings plan. Maybe it's just $50 a month or $100, but start now. If your workplace has a pre-tax retirement plan sign up to contribute as soon as possible, and if the employer matches your contribution, maximize the match. Lastly, set a specific goal to have at least three and preferably up to six months of living expenses saved.

HABIT FOUR: GIVE GENEROUSLY

You've most likely heard of tithing; giving the first ten percent of your income to God. However, that is not all that is meant by generosity. You can give generously of your time, your talent, and your treasure. Try paying the bridge toll for the car behind you, or pay for the coffee of the person behind you in line at your local coffee shop! It's not only good for the recipient, it's good for the giver! Neuro-economists have found that, "Generosity makes people happier, even if they are only a little generous. People who act solely out of self-interest are less happy. Merely promising to be more generous is enough to trigger a change in our brains that makes us happier."[86] *"Remember this: Whoever sows sparingly will also reap sparingly, and whoever sows generously will also reap generously. Each man should give what he has decided in his heart to give, not reluctantly or under compulsion, for God loves a cheerful giver."* 2 (Corinthians 9:6-7 NIV)

> Generosity makes people happier, even if they are only a little generous.

Action Step – Consider these generous acts: If you attend a church, give there first and make it automatic (via payroll deduction, bank transfer, or text-to-give if they are so enabled.) Next, find a charitable cause you are passionate about and give with some combination of your time, talents, or treasure. Last, be aware of potential situations where your generosity can spill-out and give when it feels right!

THE CHALLENGE
Choose at least ONE of the "Action Steps" provided in this chapter and act on it!

TO THINK ABOUT...
1. How do I feel about my finances right now? Are the challenges presented in this chapter something I need to act on right now?

2. As I look back on the Scripture listed in this chapter what stands out to me?

3. Is there a cause or issue I am passionate about that I would like to contribute to with either my time, talent, or finances?

Chapter 18

STORMY WEATHER AHEAD

Are you Prepared?

By Kristen Crichton

The scene in Acts 27 opens on a ship at sea and our hero, a prisoner named Paul, was being transported to stand trial. The journey seemed to be going well, when suddenly the ship was caught in a storm of hurricane force. The ship was so violently battered by the storm that the chances of survival seemed bleak. Despite their best efforts, the crew became despondent as the storm continued to rage for fourteen days and they gave up all hope of being saved. In the midst of the storm an angel of the Lord appeared to Paul and assured him that not one person on the ship would be lost; only the ship itself would be destroyed. *"So keep up your courage, men,"* Paul advised his captors, *"for I have faith in God that it will happen just as He told me."* (v.25) And it did.

As we continue reading, we learn that while in fact the ship was run aground and broken to pieces, all 276 passengers *"reached land safely."* (v.44) How is it that while everyone around him had given up hope for survival, Paul was able to believe that they would be saved? In today's world, how is it that some people come through trials and seem to thrive, while others barely survive? As both a counselor and survivor myself, I am often asked this question. I believe that the answer to this question is absolutely critical to the Christian life.

My own personal storm lasted fourteen years. I was "caught" in a storm of a marriage to a man who suffered from mental illness and who was at times, angry and threatening to my children and to me. The marriage ended when he became violent with me, but our storm wasn't over. His anger at the loss of his family drove him to do the unthinkable. In April of 2015 he made an attempt on the lives of our young children. I fully believe that God saved their lives that day. But the true miracle was that not only were we saved, we walked away from the ordeal stronger than ever. Why? Because we were equipped to endure the storm.

STORM WARNING

In John chapter 16 Jesus warns His disciples of the trials that they can expect as they live out the Christian life in a fallen world. *"I have told you all this so that you may have peace in me. Here on earth you will have many trials and sorrows. But take heart, because I have overcome the world!"* (John 16:33 NLT) That is a statement of fact. As Christians we *will* have trials. So why is it that so often we are surprised when adversity strikes? Many Christians throw up their hands in frustration and cry, "I wasn't ready for this! How could something like this happened to me? How could God *let* this happen?" Yet what we must understand is that trials come both because of our humanity and because of our identity in Christ. So, if we know this to be true what shall we do? The same thing we would do at this moment if we heard on the news that a storm was coming: We need to BE PREPARED!

STEP ONE: TRUSTING IN A SOVEREIGN GOD

Jesus tells us that He provides this forewarning of stormy weather ahead *"so that [we] might have peace."* Additionally, he encourages us that we can have hope to endure the trials by remembering *"I have overcome the world!"* Peace and hope are possible only by remembering *who* is ultimately in control.

Our son-in-law, Parker, an Air Force pilot, once took our family flying while we were on vacation. While I was peacefully enjoying the coastal views Parker's voice came over the headphones. "Hold on!" he teased as he pulled back on the yoke, sending the plane straight up into the sky! For several minutes the plane twisted and looped through the skies in a demonstration of aerobatics. I begged him to stop as Parker suddenly placed the little plane into stall-out situation and we began careening to the earth. Falling I felt so vulnerable and out of control. No matter what I did, I could not save myself. Yet strangely I had peace, knowing that our lives rested in Parker's capable hands. I knew without a doubt that he would deliver us safely back onto the ground as he had done thousands of times before.

This is exactly what Jesus meant in John 16:33. It is as if we are flying through the skies with Jesus as our pilot and He says "Hold on tight, this flight is about to get bumpy, but don't worry, I have flown these skies a thousand times before and am confident that I will get you to your destination. Trust me."

As we surrender and recognize that we cannot endure the trials and sorrows by our own strength, we begin to place ourselves in God's capable hands.

STEP TWO: BUILDING A COMMUNITY

Two days after I got out of the hospital after being nearly beaten to death by my (then) husband I got a call from my pastor. "Kristen, I'm getting phone calls from so many people wanting to know how they can help you and your family. Would you be willing to come to the church tonight to share with everyone what it is you are needing right now and how we can support you?"

When I arrived at church that night I walked into a room full of friends and family. Tears and hugs flowed freely as we clung to one another in a state of shock and uncertainty. I shared my story while my church community surrounded me in prayer and then stepped up and offered their help to my broken little family. Someone asked our pastor if he had had many opportunities to gather believers in this way around someone in the midst of trauma. He shook his head and said, "Sadly, no. This is the first time. There aren't many people who will open themselves up and be willing to be this vulnerable with others." It was because I invited the support of my community that we were able to persevere through the darkest days of our life. God didn't take our trials or sorrows away. Instead, He surrounded us with a community to help meet our needs and to strengthen us for the journey.

STEP THREE: HOPING IN THINGS UNSEEN

Every year my new husband and I participate in a 100K cycling event that requires months of training. One year my leg cramped up as we hit mile fifty just before a difficult two-mile uphill climb. "I can't make it Lord!" I cried. In truth, there was no other option. I had to climb, never mind the pain. Trusting that God would somehow get me up the hill, I prayed for strength and endurance as tears of pain streamed from my eyes. Yet, rather than strengthening, my leg began to spasm.

> God didn't take our sorrows away...He surrounded us with community.

Suddenly I felt a hand upon my back, pushing me up the hill. Glancing back I saw my husband, straining as he pedaled us both slowly up the hill. "Just keep pedaling," he directed. I found myself pedaling with greater ease, as he pushed. "You got this!" cyclists called out. I now had hope to push through the pain to reach the top and finish the ride.

I realized that day how this moment was like life. We have a responsibility to prepare for what lies ahead. However, what we cannot ignore is that *our* training will never be enough, because God never intended that we would shoulder our greatest burdens alone. God answered my prayer that day in an unexpected way. He didn't take away the pain. He restored my hope so I could endure.

An important part of walking in faith is that we must hope in the unknown, the unseen. Romans 8:24 reminds us that "*...hope that is seen is no hope at all. Who hopes for what they already have?*" What is it that we are placing our hope and trust in? It is what we cannot see. It is the confidence that "*our light and momentary troubles are achieving for us an eternal glory that far outweighs them all.*" (2 Corinthians 4:17 NIV) For me, that meant hoping in the promise that God had a plan for greater good, and He did. Just months after nearly losing their lives even my children, at the tender ages of eight and ten, were able to express thanks to God for the trial they went through. In the midst of the storm, we could never have known what God would accomplish. Yet when we set our eyes on Him, trusting Him to continue the work He has begun in us, we began to see the beauty of His plan unfolding.

THE CHALLENGE

Consider the circle of friends you have in your life right now. What are you currently doing to help spur your friends on as they face the trials and sorrows of their lives? What can you do to provide more practical support for those who may be in need? Find a person in crisis within your sphere of influence and make a decision to do something practical to help ease their burden. Ideas might include making a meal, offering childcare, mowing a lawn, paying a utility bill or offering to change the oil in their car. You may never know the encouragement your small act of kindness may provide!

TO THINK ABOUT...

1. How do I feel about the "fact" that I can expect trials and sorrows in my life as I follow Christ?

2. What are some things that God has done for me in the past that I will need to remember in order to encourage me when I am struggling to trust Him to get me through?

3. What is a Bible verse that I could memorize that I can put on "repeat" in my mind as I am striving to persevere through trials?

Chapter 19

STRESS

Our Close Friend...What?

By Melanie Trowbridge

I bet this apparent friendship nonsense got your attention! Yep, it's no typo. Stress is something that each of us knows all too well. Maybe it takes the form of family or friend drama, assignment deadlines, or a draining busy schedule. Stress is often a visitor whether you've invited it in or not. However, how often do you view stress as positive? When you size it up, how does its 'cons' list compare with its 'pros' list? If you put a face to it, does it look more like Mary Poppins, the crisp motivator, or Pooh's anxious and flustered buddy, Piglet? Here's my invitation to you. Let's take a few moments together and consider some of the possible items on that pros list.

NAME IT!

Let's get on the same page and land on what we mean when we use the word "STRESS". Stress is how our brain and body respond to any demand.[87] Every type of demand (or stressor) such as school, work, exercise, sickness, or major life changes can be stressful. Any of these can result in our 'perceived' disconnect between a situation and our resources to deal with that situation. That is why people cope with stressors differently, and why some cope with demand more effectively or recover more quickly than others.

NEED IT?

Why do we need to experience stress at all...considering all the possible downsides to this seemingly slippery quicksand that can swallow us alive if we are not careful? Three important words, *stress is useful!* I would go so far as to suggest that without it, you and I would not be having this discussion, nor would you be interested in reading this book either out of curiosity or for insight.

Ponder for a moment the following "what-if". What

> *Three important words...*
> *Stress is useful.*

if you had never experienced any stress (demand) in all of your years of K-12 educational homework and assignments? Quite possibly, you might now be finding that your preparation and training for career success was inadequate. So, stress can be our ally, even our friend, because it keeps us accountable for our behaviors. It motivates us into action.

Can we agree, at times our overwhelming feelings in response to stressors can be paralyzingly uncomfortable? Yet, stress also forces us to problem solve. Problem solving can encourage growth by building our confidence and resilience. When these increase, we tend to feel less threatened and more in control of our situations.

THE FLIP SIDE

What if, despite encouragement to face the demand, we instead choose to avoid it? Choosing to avoid the stressor that makes us feel uncomfortable can actually teach us to continue a pattern of avoidance. But if we face the challenging stressor and work through the experience, we are likely to be more equipped to handle similar challenges in the future. The process is habit forming.

Medical studies have found that appropriate doses of stress (moderate levels of daily stress) are not only psychologically helpful but physically can help to protect us against certain aging and disease processes by boosting the immune system.[88] Yet if the stress response is *not managed*, our bodies can suppress our immune system, and cause digestive, headache, sleep, and mood problems. Over time, the demands that stress generates can contribute to more serious illnesses such as depression, anxiety, diabetes, high blood pressure, and heart disease.

WHO DECIDES THE POWER OF IT?

You do! Remember, when we began our conversation we agreed to define STRESS as our reaction to that demanding stressor...that disconnect between the demand and our resources to deal with that demand. That opens up the possibility that stress could be a real or imagined alert that is taxing our available resources. For example, let's say that you and I are in a group who has signed up to sky dive. For some of us (me), this is an intimidating and stress-inducing experience. For others (maybe you), this is an exhilarating proposition. Thus, our individual 'perception' of sky diving can influence our stress response.

If we perceive something as stressful, our brains release chemical messages that influence our behavior, mental experience, and physical functioning. If the stressor is real and requires action, the chemical messages will allow us to behave appropriate to the risk. What if the stressor is largely a function of our invention, such as my distress about being given a faulty parachute? Well, the same chemical messages are sent into action. If the imagined stressor is chronic, thinking about a whole semester of sky diving outings using faulty equipment, then over time these chemical messages can cause the brain and body to actually change. It is the kind of reorganizational change that can lead to problems.

> The fact that stress is a perceptions means we can do something about it.

The good news is the reorganization ability of our brain to form new connections as a result of those chemical messages can be positive. Our brain is wonderfully plastic. Just like a plastic water bottle. We can squeeze, squish, and stomp that plastic water bottle and still it maintains the integrity of a plastic water bottle. The same holds true for our brain. God has created this organ to compensate for significant injury and disease and to adjust its activities in response to new situations and fluctuations in environment. What does this have to do with our stress conversation? The fact that stress is a perception also means that we can do something about it! We have the choice to *train ourselves* to change our perspective. This change has the powerful capacity not only to modify perspective, but also to alter the structure and functions of our brain toward health.

Let's consider for a moment the Apostle Paul in prison. No matter where we are in our life walk, being in prison would be a stressor! Yet Paul wrote these words, *"I am not saying this because I am in need, for I have learned to be content whatever the circumstances. I know what it is to be in need, and I know what it is to have plenty. I have learned the secret of being content in any and every situation, whether well fed or hungry, whether living in plenty or in want. I can do all this through him who gives me strength."* (Philippians 4:12-13 NIV) Notice Paul's use of the word "learned". Managing stressors often requires us to "learn" or practice a new approach on how to change our perspective. Paul changed his view on life circumstances and saw reality through a perspective God provided.

One way to transform our perspective about stress is to change the situation. Let's use a very real and daily demand that many of us face…commuting. If my commute is causing some white knuckle, heart-pounding reactions, can I modify my commute logistics to ease that disconnect between the stressor and my available resources to deal with the stressor? Could I change the timing or route chosen? Another way to transform our perspective about stress is to change the way we view the situation. For instance, if I cannot significantly change my commute, can I re-focus the drive time into listening to entertaining or educational podcasts instead? Some stress may be inevitable, but we have some deliberate influence in whether it will result in plastic brain changes that can harm or help. By amending the way I interpret and interact with the stressors and demands around me, I gain control over my stress. By changing my perspective on each stressor and how I interact with it, I change my brain toward health.[89]

CHALLENGE

We've considered that a life without stress isn't necessarily a better life. For example, I am fairly certain that resilience is a character goal you and I would both appreciate owning. That character product is not easy to come by, but requires the ingredients of demands or stressors that allow us to "learn" the goal. Galatians 6:9 encourages us with *"let us not grow weary while doing good, for in due season we shall reap if we do not lose heart."* (NKJV)

Many times that of which we are most proud and brings the most meaning in our lives is a result of facing demand with effort. If you were to wipe out the stressors and accompanying stress in your life, would you also wipe away much of the meaning in some of your life's achievements? The challenge is to appreciate motivating stress and transform either our view of, or the stressor itself that is defeating. Finally, we can recognize that both the appreciation and the transforming processes are "learned" behaviors!

TO THINK ABOUT...

1. How can stress be a healthy part of my life?

2. How might interpreting and interacting with stressors take on a healthier approach for me?

3. What current stressor might I change by transforming the stressing situation or the way I view it?

4. What else do I need to explore on this topic? Are there other chapters in the book that can help?

Chapter 20

THE GIANTS OF ANXIETY & DEPRESSION

When Stress is NOT Our Friend

By Melanie Trowbridge

Before you start this chapter flip back and read chapter 19. Now that we have a proper backdrop, let's consider a typical morning ritual. After a late night of assignment deadlines and three loads of laundry, you're feeling a bit of relief the moment you extract yourself from traffic and slip into the coffee house drive-through lane. With pleased anticipation, you order your favorite large caramel macchiato. *What? They're out of syrup! How depressing!* As you slink back into traffic holding your paltry mocha, you're anxiously convinced that this must be code for a miserable day ahead.

LABEL CONUNDRUM

How often do we hear or use those words…"depressed" and "anxious" and "stress"? They are familiar labels tossed into our daily conversations. In fact, if you ask others to name common mental health concerns, chances are *anxiety* and *depression* will likely via for the top two spots. Despite the fact that these two "emotional experiences" are commonly referenced in our dialogue more than ever, many of us struggle in our understanding of what these words really involve. It's no wonder. We use these labels as one-word descriptors to communicate so many experiences. But labels can be misleading especially when they are used to describe common life events as well as diagnostic categories... anything from a morning coffee debacle to months of crippling psychological pain. *I'm so depressed that I missed out on my caramel macchiato today.* Contrast this with the following. *My depression is getting rough...I'm sad all the time, I can't sleep much, and my energy and concentration are poor.* Both individuals likely experience distress, yet the severity and length of time of each of their experiences admittedly hold a different value. To complicate things further, stress, anxiety, and depression often share some of the same symptoms. From the outside looking in, it can be difficult to spot the differences.

LABEL CLARITY
Our fingertip-ready information age is ever willing to lend a hand with definitions, statistics, and personal experiences regarding anxiety, depression, and stress. Reliable material is valuable in helping us to shape our understanding of and our response to these sometimes confusing labels. The American Psychiatric Association and the American Psychological Association are two reliable sources rich with information for you to explore. I'd like to spend just a bit of time with you on these labels but encourage you to visit these resources.

In the last chapter we looked at stress in detail. The limelight was positioned on stress's positive side. Because stress is a response to a threat or demand in any given situation, it can help us pull off that deadline you thought was a lost cause. While stress can be a friend, it can often be a foe when it overextends its welcome. While stress can manifest in various negative ways, it can be helpful to be aware of some likely symptoms:[90]

- Irritability
- Headaches
- Sleep disturbance
- Muscle tension or pain
- Frequent illness
- GI problems
- Dizziness or light-headed
- Feeling overwhelmed
- Forgetfulness
- Low energy
- Worry
- Poor concentration

There are a number of recognized emotional and physical disorders linked to stress. Stress often delivers an unwelcomed contribution for anxiety and/or depressive disorders. Let's begin with anxiety which is a persistent mental health disorder that

> While stress can be a friend, it can often be a foe when it overextends its welcome.

does not fade into the background once a threat or demand is over. This clinical anxiety stays around much longer than is ever comfortable and can cause significant impairment in social, occupational, biological, and other important areas of functioning. There are many disorders where clinical anxiety displays itself. One of the most prevalent is Generalized Anxiety Disorder, where excessive anxiety and worry occurs most of the time for at least six months. The intensity of the anxiety and worry is out of proportion to the actual impact or likelihood of the anticipated event. Typical symptoms include:[91]

- Difficulty controlling worry
- Restlessness or on edge
- Easily fatigued
- Difficulty concentrating
- Irritability
- Muscle tension
- Sleep disturbance
- Exaggerated startle response
- Psychosomatic symptoms: Headaches, stomachaches, dizziness, pins and needles
- Physical symptoms: Shortness of breath, rapid heartbeat, excessive sweating, shortness of breath, chest pain
- The anxiety, worry, or physical symptoms cause clinically significant distress or impairment in social, occupational, or other areas of functioning

Clinical depression is another sustained mental health disorder. Despite the easy use of its title in our conversations, it can be anything but easy in its character. It is far more than feeling sad. Indeed, everyone feels down or unmotivated from time to time, but clinical depression is much more serious. It is a mood disorder characterized by extended feelings of sadness and significant loss of interest in daily activities that affects the body, thoughts, and behavior. There is no single cause or single type of depression. Just as clinical anxiety expresses itself in different ways, so too does clinical depression. However, there are similar recognizable symptoms. Some of these include:[92]

- Persistent feelings of sadness, hopelessness, worthlessness, or emptiness
- Irritability, frustration, or restlessness
- Loss of interest in activities or hobbies that used to be enjoyable
- Difficulty sleeping, sleep disturbances, or sleeping too much
- Fatigue and lack of energy
- Difficulty thinking clearly, remembering, concentrating, or making decisions
- Appetite or weight changes
- Recurrent thoughts of death or suicide
- Physical symptoms such as headaches, stomachaches, or back pain

I'm sure you've already spotted a handful of symptoms that cross over into two or even all three of our labels. For instance, all three can produce sleepless nights, fatigue, lack of focus and headaches. With symptoms that can appear interchangeable, it can be difficult to know when to work on deep breathing and when it's time to seek appropriate help. A good rule of thumb is when the signs or symptoms like those listed no longer feel manageable and interfere with your daily living, it's time to seek help from an appropriate mental health provider. And while stress has its pros and cons lists, the clinical diagnoses of anxiety and depression favor the con list. Good news…anxiety, depression, and unhealthy stress are all very treatable. Remember that plastic water bottle word picture we discussed in the last chapter, the sooner we begin treatment, the sooner we facilitate changing our brain toward health!

A VERBAL PICTURE WORTH A THOUSAND WORDS

Proverbs encourages us to seek wise counsel. Wise counsel can come in forms such as credible resources, professional health care providers, as well as insightful peers. The strategic sharing of personal interactions with mental illnesses such as anxiety or depression has the power to educate, reduce stigma, decrease fear, and lessen shame. The following picture is adapted from a patient of mine who has given consent to share their story. Her hope is to encourage and support you as you learn to either encourage yourself or a loved one.

I've been battling with anxiety and depression most of my short life. One reason that my early years were so much of a struggle can be summed up in this phrase: 'Get closer to God and your faith will treat your problems'. I agree that my relationship with Jesus is most important, but it just made me angry at God to hear these types of phrases because I wasn't making any progress. It was like I was a prisoner of my own thoughts, and I wasn't allowed to feel the way I was feeling.

My parents finally took me to see a psychiatrist but refused to let her prescribe medication at first. Things started to escalate in college. Even though I found a support system of amazing friends that encouraged me and reassured me that what I was feeling was not all within my willpower to control. They, and my psychiatrist, helped me build the courage to confront others' misunderstandings about my mental health and educate them that I needed a similar kind of help as someone who struggles with chronic asthma or diabetes. I also needed Jesus to help me see I needed to live a healthy lifestyle, and finally to accept that I needed help from outside of myself including medication, educational programs, and therapy.

My parents, my church, and I see that having a strong faith and relationship with Jesus is a very necessary answer to mental health. We also now realize that Jesus created me to care for not only my relationship with Him but my relationship with my body and my mind. For me, this means ongoing mental health treatment. Everyone's support literally saved my life. Anxiety and depression are everyday battles, but the support of those around me has made it a lot easier.

THE CHALLENGE

The month of May is designated as Mental Health Awareness Month. However we should never wait for May to discuss and consider actions on such a powerful topic! The following statistics ought to challenge us toward improving how we identify, understand, and respond to mental health disorders in general, but especially the two most prevalent...anxiety and depression.

In the USA, approximately half of us will experience a mental illness during our lifetime. Half of these mental disorders begin by age fourteen and three-quarters by age twenty-four. In the USA, only 41 percent of those with a mental disorder in the past year sought help.[93]

Consider the impact. Can these statistics encourage positive behavior on your part?

TO THINK ABOUT...
1. How can my ongoing increased understanding of mental health disorders positively affect: Me? Others? My relationships with others?

2. There is now less stigma around mental illness, but more can be done. What role could I play in addressing the stigma?

3. What accompanying chapters in this book give me tools as I think about the questions above?

Chapter 21

WHEN JUST A FRIEND WON'T DO

It's Time for the Big C

By Meghan McMahon Johnson

Before I jump into what the "Big C" is, I would first like to you ponder two questions. The first is, "What are friends for?" Take a few minutes to think about that. Grab a piece of paper and split it in two. On one side write out your answers to the question "What are friends for?" On the other side write "Friends are not", we'll get to that portion in a moment.

FRIENDS ARE FOR...

If I were to answer that question myself, my chart would look something like this...With friends I feel support. We have fun, laugh, and cry together. My friends challenge me, comfort me, and we can take off and explore the world. Unconditional love, prayer, and late night coffee runs describe my friendships. Friends are here to worry about me, care for me, and cover for me when needed (and I for

Friends are for...	Friends are not...

them). We sneak out together, fall asleep in front of the TV, and when the all else fails go dancing. With friends I share my darkest secrets, complain about life, I can be sad, angry and occasionally we just sit in silence. Friends are here for a plethora of situations in our lives! However, have you considered what friends are *not* here for?

FRIENDS ARE NOT...

Take few minutes now and fill out the side labeled "Friends are not..." This section might not be as easy to fill out as the first part or maybe it is. I guess much of that depends on the nature of the friendships you have experienced in the past or the friendships you are currently navigating. What roles are friends *not* to play? Your answers might include, friends are not to be...the sole source of comfort in my life, the answer to all my problems, a rescuer to save me from difficulties, or expected to be there physically or emotionally *all the time*.

When we think of friendships, we often focus on the positive aspects of what friendship brings. However, there are also negative aspects to friendships we need to consider. Ponder this, are the reasons you listed simply character flaws or *unjust expectations that we place on friendships*?

THE BIG C!

Counseling. Yup, I said it. Counseling. Don't turn the page, lean in a little closer if you can. Say it with me...counseling. Did you shudder when you said it? Did the hair stand up on the back of your neck? Did you roll your eyes at me? I hope not. However, I do understand there is a huge stigma that surrounds counseling and starting therapy. Let's take a moment to break it all down.

What is counseling? Counseling is a professional relationship that empowers diverse individuals, families, and groups to accomplish mental health, wellness, and education and career goals.[94] As a breathing, living definition, counseling can look different based on the needs of each individual. Counseling is not one size fits all. It does not look or feel the same for everyone. Probably one of the best aspects of counseling is that it is designed to fit what *you* need in that moment. Counseling is not a quick fix. It takes time, dedication, and commitment to your goals to see the benefits of counseling. Let me give you a few statistics.

Approximately 43.8 million adults experience a mental illness. One in five children ages 13-18 have, or will have a serious mental illness. Half of all lifetime cases of mental illness will begin by age 14 and 75% by age 24.[95] There is approximately a 6-8 year delay in seeking treatment for mood disorders and 9-23 year delay in seeking treatment for anxiety disorders.[96] A whopping 70-90% of individuals reported improved quality of life after receiving support and treatment.[97]

If we break that down, what does the data mean in plain English? It means that you or someone you know will most likely experience some sort of mental illness and will be more likely not to seek help, despite research showing that help works.

If we "*know*" that counseling works, why is it that more people do not go? In my experience working with college students in a Student Care department, I find some very common answers to that question. First, I can barely pay for school and counseling costs too much. Second, I hardly have time to study let alone time for counseling. Third, it would be weird to talk to someone I do not know. Finally, the last one and maybe most interesting one of all is; I would rather just talk to my friends who I know I can trust. Let's think about that in relation to the questions I asked at the beginning of the chapter, what friends are for and what roles our friends should not take.

THE COUNSELOR'S JOB

Let me start this off by making this point very clear; *friends are not our counselors.* I repeat: Friends are not our counselors! Here is why. Many times our friends are just not equipped to handle some of the very heavy issues that

> *If we know that counseling works, why is it more people do not go?*

we have to navigate. Having a therapeutic relationship is more than just a support system it also provides you the opportunity to talk to a confidential resource that is trained to listen to you. It is literally the job of the counselor to listen to what you are saying and help guide you in exploring the root or source of the problems. Counselors equip us with tools and techniques to better manage our emotions, improve relationships, identify negative thought patterns, and help us understand more authentically who we are.

If we are being honest with one another, friends can be flaky. We know they mean well but sometimes their own lives take precedence over ours. Even a good friend might not answer when we call. If they do answer they may rush us off the phone with a sincere but light-hearted "It'll be alright, don't worry." Sometimes they just may not have any words for us at all. It is in those moments that I challenge you to explore how counseling might change the trajectory of your life.

You can approach this from two perspectives; as someone who may be considering contacting a counselor because talking to friends is no longer helping, or as someone who may need to encourage a friend to go see a counselor because *you* do not have the words to help. In either case here are three steps to take. Pray that God might reveal what He would want you to do. Talk to a trusted friend about the desire to seek out counseling. Finally get some recommendation of good local counselors that you can contact when you are ready.

BE EMPOWERED

Here is my final thought to help bring this all together. I love how Ephesians 4 reads.

> *"Now these are the gifts Christ gave to the church: the apostles, the prophets, the evangelists, and the pastors and teachers. Their responsibility is to equip God's people to do his work and build up the church, the body of Christ. This will continue until we all come to such unity in our faith and knowledge of God's Son that we will be mature in the Lord, measuring up to the full and complete standard of Christ. Then we will no longer be immature like children. We won't be tossed and blown about by every wind of new teaching. We will not be influenced when people try to trick us with lies so clever*

they sound like the truth. Instead, we will speak the truth in love, growing in every way more and more like Christ, who is the head of his body, the church.[16] *He makes the whole body fit together perfectly. As each part does its own special work, it helps the other parts grow, so that the whole body is healthy and growing and full of love."* (Ephesians 4:11-16 NLT)

Christ gave each of us special gifts. Our responsibility is to use each of these gifts to build up the body of Christ (each other). An apostle is an apostle not a prophet. A teacher is a teacher not an evangelist. Each gift, in order to be effective and maximize its potential, has to flow in the area it was designed to do. This is the same for friendships. Friends are here to just be our friends, not our counselors. When just a friend won't do, *be empowered* to seek help from professionals who are willing, ready, and able to listen.

> *Friends are here to be our friends, not our counselors.*

THE CHALLENGE

Be honest with yourself. Is it time for the Big C? If you decide that it is, remember that counseling is private, unbiased, and offers a safe space to dissect our innermost thoughts, feelings, emotions, and experiences and leave us feeling refreshed, encouraged, and equipped to take on another day.

TO THINK ABOUT...
1. What stands out to me in the chapter?

2. Have I been using my friends as counselors when perhaps I need something more?

3. Which of the three steps listed above do I need to pursue if I think I need to see a counselor?

Chapter 22

ANY SECOND NOW

Persevering Through Problems

By Thomas Fitzpatrick

Half a second.

Unless you are talking about bull riding or the 40-yard dash, that's not much time at all. Half a second is literally the blink of an eye or the snap of a finger. And, half a second is all it takes to transition from Matthew 14:25 to Matthew 14:26. Try it. Read the text for yourself.

> *Immediately Jesus made the disciples get into the boat and go on ahead of him to the other side, while he dismissed the crowd. 23 After he had dismissed them, he went up on a mountainside by himself to pray. Later that night, he was there alone, 24 and the boat was already a considerable distance from land, buffeted by the waves because the wind was against it. 25 Shortly before dawn Jesus went out to them, walking on the lake. 26 When the disciples saw him walking on the lake, they were terrified. "It's a ghost," they said, and cried out in fear. 27 But Jesus immediately said to them: "Take courage! It is I. Don't be afraid."* (Matthew 14:22-27 NIV)

I told you. Moving from one verse to the next here in Matthew 14 happens in a flash, and it is probably the easiest thing you will do all day (you can thank me later). In verse 24, the disciples are in trouble. In verse 25, Jesus comes to the rescue. Half a second to move from one verse to the next and suddenly the conflict is resolved.

However, here's the thing. It took longer, A LOT longer in fact, for the events in this chapter to unfold in real time. Half a second – not even close. Half an hour – if only. Half the afternoon – still not long enough. The disciples had to struggle against seemingly insurmountable obstacles for nearly half a day – twelve full hours.

That is what makes this particular story so important and so impactful. It is a story about great perseverance and trust. It is a story about not giving up and not giving in. It is a story about keeping your eyes up even when the world tries to beat you down. It is a story that many of us can relate to and a story from which many of us need to learn.

> It is a story about keeping your eyes up even when the world tries to beat you down.

A little context behind the story will help. Earlier in Matthew 14, we read that Jesus and the disciples miraculously fed 5000 people with nothing more than a little boy's brown bag lunch. I imagine that would have been one of the most exhilarating, yet exhausting, experiences to say the least. So when we get to verse twenty-two, we shouldn't be surprised when Jesus asks the disciples for a little "alone time" (and all of the introverts in the room said 'amen')! Jesus specifically asked that the disciples go ahead of him, across the Sea of Galilee, so that He could be alone with the Father in prayer.

Don't miss that. *Jesus* sent the disciples away. *He* told them to go out on the sea alone. *He* put them out on the water all by themselves. All of this was *His* idea and *His* doing. Which must have made what happened next to the disciples that much harder to handle.

REAL LIFE
Within an hour or two of being out on the sea, a huge storm rolls over the water and starts to beat against the disciple's boat, as well as their beliefs. They fight against the wind and the waves, as well as for their very lives, hour after hour after hour. Twelve hours in fact.

Matthew provides us with a few different time stamps that are easy to miss but critically important to the story. Jesus dismissed the crowd and sent the disciples to the boat. It was well before the sun had even set, probably somewhere around 6pm., and the dark clouds had already rolled in.

Jesus doesn't show up until the "forth watch of the night". That phrase doesn't make a whole lot of sense to us because our iPhones or Android devices don't track time that way (*Siri, set a timer for the fourth watch of the night*). However, back in the first century, the fourth watch of the night was somewhere between 3am and 6am.

The disciples most likely started fighting against this storm at 6pm. And Jesus didn't show up until perhaps 6am! That's 12 hours. Think about that for a moment...for 12 hours the disciples are alone fending for themselves on the open seas. For 12 hours they have to exert all the energy they can muster to stay afloat and to stay alive. For 12 hours they have to worry and wonder about their well-being and their worth. Twelve hours seems like a long time, imagine an exhilarating day at Disneyland with friends. It is an even longer time when you are fighting against the storms of life.

I love the way author Max Lucado describes this scene,

> "Imagine the incredible strain of bouncing from wave to wave in a tiny fishing vessel. One hour would weary you. Two hours would exhaust you. Surely Jesus will show up to help. But he doesn't. Their arms being to ache from the rowing. Still no sign of Jesus. Three hours. Four hours. The winds rage. The boat bounces. Midnight comes. Their eyes search for God, in vain. 1am. 2am. 3am. The hours feel like days. All this time they have fought the storm and sought the master. And so far, the storm is winning and the Master is nowhere to be found." [98]

I'm sure many of us can relate to this feeling. We followed Jesus to where we sensed He was calling us, and now, well now we are really struggling and totally stressed out. We took a step of faith and walked in obedience, and now we are in a situation that is causing us to doubt or question our faith.

Have you ever asked yourself questions like...

God, what were you thinking?

God, where in the world are you?

God, why are you allowing this to happen to me?

I certainly have. I know what it feels like to be suspended between verses 24 and 25, from relationships to professional pursuits to struggles against certain sins and temptations. I know what it feels like to be "buffeted" by the waves, hour after hour after hour, not sure of what the future will hold or if I have what it takes to make it through. I know what it's like to feel as if Jesus has abandoned me and left me on the water to die. Although it only takes half a second to get to the "Jesus saving" ending when you read the story, it takes much longer to get to that point in real life. For some of us, the transition has not happened yet. We are still in verse 24, unsure of whether or not verse 25 will ever come.

THE CHALLENGE

Although I can't say with absolute certainty what "watch of the night" you are in, or how much longer you might have to wait or work or wonder, I do know this: At any second Jesus could show up. At any second, the One who calls the stars out by name,

> *At any second, the problem that feels like it will go on forever, will suddenly be over.*

could call out your name. At any second, the One who created the wind and the waves, could calm those very same things in your life. At any second, the problem that feels like it will go on forever, will suddenly be over. That's how it was for the disciples. After twelve long, grueling hours, Jesus showed up and changed everything. Just like the storm itself, Jesus showed up so unexpectedly. And the same will be true for you.

You just need to keep fighting. You just need to keep rowing. You just need to keep hoping.

"We can rejoice, too, when we run into problems and trials, for we know that they help us develop endurance. And endurance develops strength of character, and character strengthens our confident hope of salvation. And this hope will not lead to disappointment. For we know how dearly God loves us, because he has given us the Holy Spirit to fill our hearts with his love." (Romans 5:3-5 NIV)

Ever face a problem? The Bible says it is actually a tool to help you develop perseverance. Ever struggle with something? The Bible says it is something that can make you stronger. Ever encounter a hardship? The Bible says that very thing can solidify your hope! God promises that our hope "will NOT lead to disappointment." Read that promise again. You *will not* be disappointed when you put your hope in the Lord.

At any second, Jesus is going to show up and free you from your fears and save you from your storms. At any second, Jesus is going to show up and calm the chaotic waters. At any second, everything will be totally different. So don't lose heart. Don't lose hope. The dawn of a new day is most likely just half a second away.

TO THINK ABOUT...
1. What storm am I currently facing (or fighting against)? How long has it been this way?

2. Have I been tempted to "give up" or just "give in"? Why or why not?

3. How does the hope that Jesus could show up at any second help me persevere?

4. What parts of Romans 5:3-5 stand out/speak to me today? Spend some time pressing into and reflecting on that verse and allow God to speak to you through it.

Chapter 23

DON'T GET BURNED...OUT

Beating Busyness & Burnout

By Fritz Moga

Before we talk about burnout...let's talk about busyness! Busy is defined as *"engaged in action; full of activity."* How busy are you? On a scale of 1 to 10 how would you rate yourself? Let's say a 1 is laying in a hammock under a tree, ear-buds in listening to slow jazz music and 10 is well, maybe picture an octopus with something in each one of their eight tentacle-like limbs, flinging them to and fro! What number do you choose for yourself at this stage of life?

YOU WANT A PIECE OF ME?
Consider the following people or categories whose expectations might pull at your energy and time.

Friends – Friends expect you to, well, be a friend. To be with them, to go places with them or just to sit with them. It takes time and energy to be a good friend!

Family – Parents, siblings, "family time", and spouses can all be great contributors to our life or they can cause us to live under the constant fear that we will disappoint them.

School/Professors – Every professor expects the best from you. If you are in college this category takes a great amount of time currently. It won't forever, but something else, probably work, will take its place!

Job/Bosses – If you have a job now, you know that a lot is expected of you…be on time, look good, be polite to customers, work hard, don't take too many days off…and the list goes on.

Sports – Only athletes can really understand how much time it takes to train and compete, especially at the collegiate level.

Ministry/Serving – If you serve anywhere, you know that to do it well you need to be fully committed.

God – Does He want a piece of you? How does that look on a daily basis? How much time and energy does He "require" or do you sacrifice to Him?

None of these are necessarily negative but the multiple expectations build up until we find ourselves running in a dozen directions. We may sacrifice personal goals in order to "look good" as we face the "tyranny of the urgent" each day. As a result we try to become super-human to please everyone!

> "If the devil can't make you bad, he'll make you busy."

There is a syndrome called "Hurry Sickness" which is characterized by hurrying through every activity of the day just to get to the next activity.

One of my former students wrote about hurry sickness like this:

"This 'disease' has affected me by causing me to not take time for myself which causes me to be stressed more than I should be. It causes me to not get enough sleep or eat properly which causes me physical exhaustion and a propensity to become sick. These initial causes then cause stress in my relationship with my wife and co-workers, which leads to ineffective work or at least less-effective work. This causes frustration in some areas of my workplace and can affect all my relationships. Eventually I force myself to take time for myself which causes me to fall behind and create the need to hurry again."

BEWARE OF BURNOUT

If busyness is not handled in the right manner it can eventually lead to burnout. Burnout has been described as *"a state of physical, emotional and mental exhaustion marked by physical depletion and chronic fatigue, feelings of helplessness and hopelessness, and by development of a negative self-concept and negative attitudes towards work, life and other people."* [99]

There is a new word in the vocabulary of the people of Japan. It is the word *Karoshi*. It translates to *"dying from overwork."* Men in Japan are working so much they have dropped dead from it, literally. The widow gets a certificate to hang on the wall and some compensation.

I first read about this in a book called *Thrilled to Death: How the Endless Pursuit of Pleasure is Leaving us Numb* by Dr. Archibald Hart. [100] After I read this I spoke to a group of eighty high school students at a camp in northern California. Among the eighty students were twenty students and their teacher (or Sensei) from Tokyo. I asked the teacher about this word and she said, "YES it does exist." In fact there is a saying among the women in

Japan; if your husband comes home and dies in the house put him OUTSIDE your front door before you call the authorities. Then it is considered Karoshi because he apparently died BEFORE he made it home. That way you get the compensation for his death.

There are many signs you might be on the edge of burnout. A few you might want to consider are:

> *In order to beat burnout we need to go in reverse and try to get less busy!*

decreased energy, feeling like a failure, pouring into people or projects and lot feeling much of a reward, a sense of helplessness, an inability to see a way out of problems, and finally cynicism and negativity about yourself, others, work, and the world in general.[101]

BEATING BURNOUT

In order to beat burnout we need to go in reverse and try to get less busy! In essence, every chapter in this book is about beating burnout. So keep reading! Here I will just give you a quick, three-point guide to get you started.

Get Real

The reality is there will always be far too many people with expectations we just can't keep. With so many people pulling at us we must learn to balance areas in our lives. Here are just a couple to think about.

Personal Time versus Work Time. What are your primary relationships? Are you spending enough time with your friends, family members, or a spouse? If those relationships suffer because of neglect chances are your life will crumble.

Thought Time versus Activity Time. Balancing the need to study, read, and reflect, with the need to be with people and DO things creates tension. The answer is to schedule in both and stick to it. It may not look very efficient to block out a piece of your day for thinking but it may be the best and most important part of your calendar!

Get Away

I have known so many workers who brag about the long hours they work and the vacations they intentionally miss. They use lines like "I would rather burn out than rust out" and "The devil never takes a vacation, why should I?" We need to get away for mental and physical reasons. Life is not a sprint but a marathon. We will last longer when we are refreshed. Here are some MUSTS for every person:

Take days off – Walk in the woods, watch a movie, go to lunch, shop, read a book, take a nap...all of these are great options for a day off.

Take vacations – The first year at a job you may only get a week off. Take it. Vacation time generally builds up (accrues). The more years you work somewhere the more vacation time you will get. Use it! Go on a road trip, visit a friend, jump in a lake, shop at second hand stores, try an ethnic food you haven't tasted before, stop and breathe!

Take a day to plan – Go away to a quiet place and think. Where is your life going? Where would you like it

to go? What are your goals for the next week...or year?
Where does God want you to be? All these questions
need to be answered and you'll struggle to do that in the
midst of a busy office schedule and hectic paced life. Set
aside this time is to think and dream! A final prescription
for hurry sickness is...

Get with God
*"Very early in the morning, while it was still dark, Jesus got
up, left the house and went off to a solitary place, where he
prayed."* (Mark 1:35 NIV) It is interesting that this verse is
in the first chapter of the book of Mark. Mark is the book
of *Jesus' Activity*. He heals people, debates with church
leaders, appoints Apostles, and calms storms. No one
was busier than Jesus. Yet *He* took time in the early
morning to get away and be alone with God. Shouldn't
we? Enough said here...there is an entire chapter
devoted to this for your reading pleasure!

THE CHALLENGE
If you have taken the time to read this entire chapter don't
jump past this section! Perhaps it is time for a personal
audit, an inspection or examination of your life. Take
some time to sit down and review what it was that makes
you so busy. Is there something you can change? What
exactly? Start small but start with *something* and you can
avoid burnout!

TO THINK ABOUT...

1. Who "wants a piece of me"? Are they realistic expectations or not?

2. What kinds of activities do I like to do to get away the busyness of life?

3. Do I, or could I, have any support in my desire to slow down so I don't burnout? Who would it be?

4. How is my time with God? Do I need to do something in this area?

Chapter 24

BECOMING A (SELF) CARE-GIVER

Avoiding the Toxicity of Life

By Erin Ambrose

Sitting in a parked car in the back of an office building parking lot staring at a tree, may not seem like the most relaxing and rejuvenating activity, but its where I began to understand the need for self-care. As a new therapist starting to build my practice, I was working long hours and filling any open spaces in my day by reading academic journals, writing curriculum for new classes, and planning upcoming workshops. While I was able to help clients identify toxic behaviors in their lives, I was ignoring a growing toxicity in my own life: busyness! Left to my own devices, I might not have ever slowed down. Seeing clients during the day, rushing home to pick up my kids from school, helping with homework and feeding them dinner, then rushing back out to lead support groups at night, I was constantly busy. But I will never forget the evening my son, who was about nine years old at the time, looked up at me with his big blue eyes and said, "Are you leaving to help another family again tonight, Mom?" That little face looking up at me with such sadness was exactly what I needed to jolt me back to reality and help me make some drastic changes in my priorities.

Too often we can see problems in others' lives but can't see ourselves clearly. Jesus speaks of this in Matthew 7:5, *"How can you think of saying to your friend, 'Let me help you get rid of that speck in your eye,' when you can't see past the log in your own eye?"* (NLT) While I was leading workshops on having good boundaries, I had let the needs of others crowd out the needs of my family and myself. After that night I shifted my hours so I could spend more time with my family. I also started to leave my office when I had a cancelation or longer break between clients and drive my car to the back of an adjacent parking lot where there were some large redwood trees. Instead of filling the hour and my head with more information, I started allowing the Holy Spirit to fill my soul with His peace and rest. I would roll down the windows, allow the breeze to float in, perhaps listen to some worship music or read my Bible, sometimes just sit in silence and reflect on the creator of those amazing trees. Just staring at those very tall trees reminded me of God's goodness and his love for me.

> I started allowing the Holy Spirit to fill my soul with His peace and rest.

SELF-CARE IS NOT SELFISH

Questions I get asked quite frequently are, "Isn't self-care a bit selfish?" and "Doesn't the Bible say it's more blessed to give than to receive?" To those questions I say, no and yes! No, self-care isn't selfish, when it is done in the proper balance. Yes, it *is* a blessing to give to others, yet we need to take good care of ourselves in order to do that well.

The National Association of Social Workers (NASW) policy statement says that self-care is a preventative measure.[102] Chronic stress, burnout, and compassion fatigue can all result from ignoring our own needs in pursuit of caring for the needs of others. Yet all too often pastors, nurses, doctors, therapists, and caregivers of all varieties place themselves in harm's way by caring for others while not properly caring for themselves. Christians and those in full-time ministry are especially prone to feeling guilty if they say no to requests for help and end up giving more than is healthy. If left unchecked, the strain of caring for others can lead to abandonment of the ministry and in some case a full rejection of God. Our heavenly Father is not a task master who expects us to give, give, give or serve to the point of exhaustion.

Jason Hotchkiss, a board-certified chaplain, well-being researcher and adjunct professor at Cornerstone University indicates that burnout can lead to hopelessness and an inability to serve others well. In his 2018 study, he found that mindful self-care could protect against burnout and its harmful effects. He states,

> Chaplains who engaged in multiple and frequent self-care strategies experienced higher professional quality of life and low burnout risk. In the chaplain's journey toward wellness, a reflective practice of feeling good about doing good and mindful self-care are vital.[103]

When we are caring for others, we need to also care for ourselves. This isn't selfish; it's survival!

SELF-CARE IS GODLY

I have been teaching psychology for many years and I just love when a psychological truth empirically backed by research, was God's idea all along. All truth is God's truth! While this chapter could go on and on about the scientific reasons we should practice self-care, perhaps the best evidence of all can be found in the model of Jesus Christ. He practiced good self-care.

According to John's gospel, Jesus' ministry on the earth was approximately three years. While certainly we don't have knowledge of every healing miracle He performed, we do know He did other things. He went to parties, He hung out with friends and family, and often spent time in solitude. That's self-care! At a time when there were no antibiotics or modern medicine, I'm sure there was a great need for healing miracles. Jesus could have spent 24/7 of those three years working: healing people, casting out evil spirits, multiplying bread and fish. But He didn't. Jesus' life on the earth reflected a good balance of work and rest. He spent time in restorative self-care. We should too!

"After He had sent the crowds away, He went up on the mountain by Himself to pray; and when it was evening, He was there alone." (Matthew 14:23 NAS)

"After bidding them farewell, He left for the mountain to pray." (Mark 6:46 NAS)

"In the early morning, while it was still dark, Jesus got up, left the house, and went away to a secluded place, and was praying there." (Mark 1:35 NAS)

"But Jesus himself would often slip way to the wilderness and pray." (Luke 5:16 NAS)

Since Jesus took time away from caring for others to care for Himself, it makes sense for us to do that also. But Jesus got the idea from God the father.

"By the seventh day God had finished the work he had been doing; so on the seventh day he rested from all his work." (Genesis 2:2 NIV)

"But the seventh day is a sabbath to the LORD your God. On it you shall not do any work, neither you, nor your son or daughter, not your male or female servant, not your animals, nor any foreigner residing in your towns." (Exodus 20:10 NIV)

Self-care is God's idea, modeled for us in the life of Jesus Christ and we have no excuse to believe we do not need it.

SELF-CARE IS PERSONAL

We are each a unique creation and reflection of God's image. Our self-care needs and preferences will mirror the uniqueness of each one of us. Some people get recharged by being around lots of people. We call them extroverts. Introverts, however, need time away from large crowds to recharge. But many people fall somewhere in between. I'm one of those types of people. I enjoy and need time with people and time by myself. It is important for me to balance my social life with my personal time for optimal self-care.

In addition to the introversion/extroversion dynamic, activity level is another thing to consider when planning self-care. Some might prefer reading a good book, drawing, or meeting a friend for coffee. Others might enjoy going for a hike, running 5K, or playing soccer. The choices are endless! While there are countless activities that would constitute self-care, spending too much time on social media actually has been shown to drag us down instead of fill us up.[104]

> Self-care is an intentional act to restore what has been depleted by the other aspects of our life.

Self-care is an intentional act to restore what has been depleted by the other aspects of our life. It isn't selfish and is necessary for a healthy and productive life. God designed us to live a balanced life and self-care is part of that balance. Since our lives vary, our self-care will vary also. So how do you discover what your self-care should look like?

That's the fun part!

THE CHALLENGE

To discover your best self-care activities, think back to when you were a little kid. What did you enjoy doing? Try and recreate some of those things. Think outside the box! Maybe you would enjoy taking an art class? Learning to juggle? Writing a short story? Try lots of different activities and see which ones fit you the best. Let's do this!

TO THINK ABOUT...

1. How balanced is my work/school life with my downtime?

2. Do I feel guilty if I take time for me? Why?

3. How do I fill the spaces in my free time? Are they restorative?

4. What self-care activities might I enjoy?

Chapter 25

I'LL BE THERE FOR YOU

Nurturing Solid Friendships

By Mandy Schmidt

I am a self-proclaimed *Friends* (1994-2004) trivia master. I have watched the show for as long as I can remember and frequently have quotes from the characters stuck in my brain. The show does not seem very enticing; six friends that have known each other for years spend almost every day together enjoying each other's company. Yet to me, that sounds like hitting the friendship jackpot. Who doesn't want a group of people that know you extremely well, laugh together until you cry, share with you in the humdrum monotonies of life, and are present in your weakest moments? Sadly, the picture-perfect relationships of the *Friends* cast do not reflect reality. At least, they don't reflect my reality.

I have been in shallow friendships, longing for some sort of deeper conversation. I have had moments of isolation and loneliness, where all I've wanted is a friend to come alongside me, but no one was there. I have experienced pain and brokenness in friendships along with miscommunications and hurts that led to no relationship at all.

With all the heartache and difficulty that friendships can bring, why continue to pursue them? Wouldn't it be so much easier to isolate, meet our own needs, and never have to experience pain from our rejected vulnerability? I have asked myself these questions, but I've come to the conclusion that we have to keep pressing forward and pursue friendship.

You were not made to walk through life alone – you were meant to share it with others. The Creator of the Universe has woven into you a desire for connection. We see this manifested in our longing for God, for family, for a spouse, and for *friends*.

> "A real friend is one who walks in when the rest of the world walks out."
> Walter Winchell

We cannot turn away and act like we are above this need. Instead, we must press in and seek after godly friendships that will build us up in our faith, hope, and love.

WHY TOGETHER IS BETTER

The human race is inherently social. In the creation story, God declares that it is not good for man to be alone[105] and creates a wife out of Adam's side. While this story reveals beautiful truths about the intimacy and connection available in a spouse, I don't think it is intended to mean that a spouse can exclusively fulfill all our needs for connection.

Instead, I believe it is a story about the beginning of understanding that we need other individuals to thrive. Adam was perfectly okay in the garden by himself. He connected directly and intimately with God. What more could you want? However, God, in His infinite wisdom, decided that it would be better for man to exist in friendship with others.

Scripture does not only support this need for friendship – the best psychological research backs up this idea as well. A ten-year Australian study concluded that strong social networks can help you live longer.[106] An eighty-year running Harvard study supported much of the same – that our relationship satisfaction is a better predictor of a long and healthy life than our socioeconomic status, our IQ, or our DNA.[107] Can you believe that? The quality of your friendships today can have a direct impact on your health and happiness in the years to come!

God tells us it's not good for us to be alone. Research tells us it's not good for us to be alone. So what might that really look like, in our day-to-day lives?

IF JESUS HAD FRIENDS, YOU NEED THEM TOO

Our God, the Creator and Sustainer of the universe, exists in community. He exists as a trinity, manifested by Father, Son, and Holy Spirit, living in perfect unity. We see God's relational nature played out through Jesus's life. Jesus chose not to do life alone but instead created for Himself a strong network of many different friendships. He had a wide social circle and dined with tax collectors and Pharisees alike. He gathered around himself a circle of twelve committed disciples whom He walked alongside every day. Even from this twelve, He gathered an inner circle of three: Peter, James, and John. With these three disciples, He revealed the most intimate, vulnerable parts of himself that He would not share with others.

Jesus deeply loved his friends. He wept over the news of Lazarus's death, even though He planned to raise him from the dead. He washed their feet as an act of service and love. He willingly submitted to death on a cross for the sake of their salvation. Jesus's friends were incredibly valuable to Him, as evidenced by His love.

Jesus also relied on His friends. In the Garden of Gethsemane on the night before Jesus's crucifixion, Jesus asked His disciples, His friends, to stay up with Him and pray. During his crucifixion, He asked John to care for His mother after He had passed. Once raised to life, He called upon his friends to share his love and Gospel with the world.[108]

If our Lord and Savior valued friendship so much during His time on earth, then we must as well. From Jesus' example, we see that we need a strong network of others to journey alongside. We need people to rely on in our darkest hours. We need those that will commit to loving us, sharing life with us, and challenging us to pursue our faith through holding us accountable for our actions. As Jesus modeled it, so we too must follow.

FANTASTIC FRIENDS AND WHERE TO FIND THEM
So now that we can all agree that having friends is necessary, where do we go from here? In order to foster great, fulfilling friendships, first you need to find great friends. Here is a quick, three-step guide for finding and making lasting friends.

1. *Identify "safe others."*

My master's program uses this term to describe individuals that have demonstrated that they are worthy of trust. These are the people that you can be vulnerable with, confide in, and that will build you up in your walk with Christ.

When looking for a "safe other," you might want to ask questions like: Do they embody the fruit of the Spirit – love, joy, peace, forbearance, kindness, goodness, faithfulness, gentleness, and self-control? Are they positive and encouraging? Do they show individuals respect, regardless of differences and disagreements? Do they follow through on their word? Are they willing to share the truth in love?[109]

2. *Take risks.*

Everyone likes safety. It is much easier to live a predictable, insulated life confined only to your corner of comfort than to put yourself outside of your comfort zone. Nevertheless, if Scripture teaches us anything, it is that God does not intend us to live in our comfort zone – with friends or anything else.

As you pursue great friendships, take risks. Ask the other person to hang out first! Share something personal instead of wading in the shallows of conversation! Go out of your way to write a kind note or pick up a thoughtful gift! No great friendship ever came out of playing it safe. Step out from your comfort and into the unknown.

3. *Nurture the relationship.*

The church loves to talk about our need for intentionality in our relationship with God or with a spouse, but often fails to mention that it is also necessary for any friendship to thrive. Great relationships do not happen overnight. They develop over time through laughter, tears, and consistency.

> *"Friendship is born at that moment when one person says to another, 'What! You too? I thought I was the only one." C.S. Lewis*

If you want to be known, you have to spend enough time with a person so they can know you. So, pour into your relationships and prioritize them. This will only bring more depth and richness to the friendship.

THE CHALLENGE

Reach out to a friend today. It might be a step of vulnerability in inviting someone to coffee. It might be going deeper with a friend that you have kept in the shallows. In either case, be vulnerable and courageous as you try to connect.

TO THINK ABOUT...

1. How satisfied am I with my current friendships? Are my friendships deep and personal or simply shallow?

2. Are there any hurts from previous friendships that are impeding my ability to be vulnerable with current friends? Have I sought healing from those wounds?

3. Can I identify any "safe others" in my life that I would like to befriend? Is there anything that is holding me back from pursuing those relationships?

4. How can I improve as a friend? Do I identify with the traits of "safe others"? What are the areas I can grow?

Chapter 26

FROM ISOLATION TO COMMUNITY

Discovering Strength in Others

By Daniel Gluck

Perhaps Satan's chief strategy is to isolate us from community. Here, he turns our focus inward, heightens our insecurities, and slowly break us down. Messages begin to reverberate through our minds: *You'll always be alone. You'll never be enough. You're too difficult to love. You better get your act together.*

In the winter of 2003, I experienced this deep loneliness. Anxiety and depression had crippled me, and I wanted nothing more than to curl up in a dark place and waste away. A negative cloud hovered over me, and truthfully, I was difficult to love. By God's good grace and mercy, I had several people around me who continually carried me to Jesus and maintained faith that He could heal me. My wife Alyssa. Other kindred friends. Just like the men in Mark chapter 2 who broke a hole in the roof and lowered their friend to Jesus, my community walked with me and carried me to Him. Let me ask you a question: What kind of community do you have around you? Is it the kind that would stick by you when you hit rock bottom? What if you were diagnosed with a terminal illness? Or succumbed to chemical addiction? Or went through a painful divorce?

JESUS STORIES

Why did Jesus tell stories like the "Lost Sheep" and "Prodigal Son"? The shepherd almost irresponsibly leaves 99 sheep to go and find the one. How could he take such a risk? Because he knew the greater risk was isolation from community. The prodigal son, when he came to the end of himself, realized his counterfeit buddies had disappeared. Fortunately, he had a loving father to return to. A great celebration erupted when he was restored to community!

Fostering a healthy community is absolutely essential for holistic health. And while building community requires time, several practices help cultivate this kind of support network. Rather than giving you "Four Easy Steps to Community," a very Western and linear approach, I will highlight a few contrasting themes vital to thriving communities.

Dr. Grace Barnes, one of my graduate professors, used to say, "I'm a bit skeptical about the idea of 'life balance.'" Who can really keep their life perfectly poised, as if walking a tightrope at the circus? Rather, she promoted the idea of "integration." Here, the goal is to weave together complex life variables in such a way that they mesh together, like a contrapuntal melody in classical music. Instead of one central theme, multiple melodies dart back and forth, sometimes crossing, other times calling and answering. I think she was onto something.

As such, I suggest there are four key categories which, when held in tension, foster intentional, healthy community. The first pair is Authenticity and Discernment.

AUTHENTICIY AND DISCERNMENT

My grandpa Ralph was a hard-working, no-nonsense Idaho dairy farmer. Those close to him said he wasn't one to openly share emotions. He was a product of a depression-era, "never let 'em see you sweat" generation. When my dad first arrived to court his daughter, Ralph came in from the fields, gave dad a stern look-over, then without words, picked him up by the shoulders and set him aside to walk past! Yet, he was also a kind, generous, and God-loving

> "When you show up authentic, you create the space for others to do the same." Anonymous

man. Generations that are more recent have swung wildly in the opposite direction. Keeping it real, whether in relationships or on social media, has become a paramount value. Those who aren't deemed authentic are suspicious, not to be trusted. We can certainly learn from both camps.

It has long been my belief that the more authentic I can be as a person, the safer those around me will feel, and the greater the community and trust that will be established. *Authenticity breeds authenticity.* I seek to foster this in the classroom, taking special care to memorize students' names quickly, share from the heart, and so forth. Yet, I have also learned the principle of emotional intelligence in leadership. The ability to identify and manage emotions is essential, and sometimes blurting out all your feelings is neither appropriate, nor safe.

So it is with community. In order to build trust, one must take the risk of trusting. Sounds like a contradiction, doesn't it? There are people who are safe for community, and predators waiting to pounce on unsuspecting, or overly-trusting prey. Those who seek godly community work to be as authentic and sincere as possible, while establishing appropriate boundaries with "unsafe" people.

GRACE AND TRUTH

The second two principles which must be held in tension in the pursuit of community are Grace and Truth. A popular myth is that if we can just find enough people like us, then we'll have a healthy community. Not so!

We've all encountered "that guy" or "that girl" who claim they are all about the truth. *I say it like it is, and if you can't handle it, too bad!*" The problem is, no one wants to be around that person! Community necessitates truth telling, but if not tempered by grace, 'the truth' falls short.

I once had to dismiss a guy from my ministry staff. It was no fun. I still sometimes wonder if I did the right thing. Time and time again, I had offered grace when he was late, missed meetings, or failed to meet deadlines. I even sat down with him to talk about stressors and health issues that had affected his work, seeking to offer support. Despite all this, there appeared little evidence of change. Truthful community required that I have the hard conversation and let him go.

Jim Collins, in his book *Good to Great*[110] affirms that great leaders don't just surround themselves with "yes-men" and women. Rather, they build communities and organizations in which people are not afraid to speak the truth. The same is true for navigating truth and grace in the context of community. We need people around us who are for us. They will champion us in every way, but love us enough to confront us with our blind-spots.

GIVING AND RECEIVING
Giving and Receiving is the third dynamic duo for building community. One powerful lesson arose from a college mission trip to Kenya. Our college mission team had just ascended a hill in the beautiful Rift Valley countryside of Western Kenya to attend a local church service. The church building was actually an old red-brick colonial homestead where Europeans had exploited African slaves for agriculture.

Midway through the service, the African pastor stood, and in thick British-African English announced that we would celebrate communion. As we nodded in approval, several women from the church came in with bright plastic basins full of water. *What's going on?* we thought. The pastor began describing how, like Jesus at the Last Supper, their tradition was to wash one another's feet as a part of communion. Things suddenly got serious. I've got stinky missionary feet. You've got nasty Kenya feet. I guess this is happening.

In beautiful symbolism, each American student paired up with an African, knelt down, and washed one another's grimy feet – in the house of a former slave-owner! I can't think of a more poignant picture of giving and receiving. Which is easier? To wash someone *else's* feet? Or let someone wash *yours*? I suggests it's the latter. Godly community thrives when those who have excess share with those who have need, and vice versa. Both parties seek first to serve, and both parties' needs are met. This was God's intention all along.

UNITY AND DIVERSITY

The last duet is Unity and Diversity. How does one guard between welcoming diversity, and inviting division into a community? After all, *Div-ersity* and *Div-ision* both stem from the Latin root meaning "different."

I learned a profound lesson about this as a young worship leader. Tasked with assembling and shepherding several worship teams for a large Christian University, my charge was to develop bands that represented our unique community. Our school was situated in a diverse suburb of Los Angeles, and students heralded from all ethnicities and faith backgrounds. How would I "aim for the middle" to best serve our campus?

As a white male acoustic guitar player, not everyone related to my vanilla-flavored music style. I desired heterogeneity, but couldn't do it alone. The risk I took yielded an important discovery. I chose an African-American bass player, highly influenced by gospel music. My electric guitar player was Hispanic, introducing Latin flavor into our band. Our drummer was professionally trained in jazz and pop, bringing high standards of excellence. It seemed I was the weakest link. Although it required diligent work to clarify our mission, a beautiful fusion of styles resulted, creating a diverse, but cohesive worship offering. It was one of the richest experiences of my life. You might be surprised by how unity can arise from the most eclectic groups!

Seeking health in all areas of our lives demands that we pursue godly community. As Dietrich Bonhoeffer stated, this community "is not an ideal which we must realize; it is rather a reality created by God in Christ, in which we *must* participate."[111] *(Emphasis mine)* It is the mission of Christ's Kingdom that offers a unified purpose for diverse communities to embrace authenticity and discernment, grace and truth, giving and receiving, and unity and diversity.

> *"As iron sharpens iron, so one person sharpens another."* Proverbs 27:17

THE CHALLENGE

Think of three or four people who could challenge you toward godly community. Consider forming (or joining) an intentional group with them. Meet once or twice a month to share joys and challenges, pray for one another, and sharpen one another. This doesn't have to be a formal church small group or discipleship group. It could be meeting with the guys for breakfast, taking a walk or run with the girls, or joining a couple's small group. The goal is regular and intentional interaction to point each other to Jesus.

TO THINK ABOUT...

1. What is my biggest challenge with participating in community?

2. Is my tendency to be vulnerable, or guarded in community contexts? Why?

3. What types of community strengthen me? Which ones drain my energy?

4. What step might I need to take to pursue godly community today?

Chapter 27
SHARING THE JOURNEY
Finding or Being a Mentor
By Fritz Moga

Life is like a journey, a quest. We are all born into this world, placed on a path and we are on our way! It is an arduous adventure to be sure...full of incredible highs and some rock-bottom lows. There will be many good times with family and friends and most certainly areas of struggle as well. You can be sure stress, busyness and frustration will be along for the ride!

You've been on this journey for a while now and you are surrounded by people also on their own adventure. Hebrews 12:1-3 tells us,

> *"Therefore, since we are surrounded by such a great cloud of witnesses, let us throw off everything that hinders and the sin that so easily entangles. And let us run with perseverance the race marked out for us. Let us fix our eyes on Jesus, the author and perfecter of our faith, who for the joy set before him endured the cross, scorning its shame, and sat down at the right hand of the throne of God. Consider him who endured such opposition from sinful men, so that you will not grow weary and lose heart."* (NIV)

First let's look at the exhortation; *"let us run with perseverance the race marked out for us."*

Stop for just a moment and think of a movie about a journey, a race, or quest for something! What is it? Was it any of these classics? *Lord of the Rings, The Chronicles of Narnia, Harry Potter, Pirates of the Caribbean, Monte Python and the Holy Grail, The Princess Bride,* ANY Superhero film or...*The Hobbit!*

In *The Hobbit: An Unexpected Journey* (2012) the wizard Gandalf invites a reluctant Bilbo Baggins into a quest to reclaim the lost Dwarf Kingdom of Erebor from the fearsome dragon Smaug. Gandalf shares the truth that safety on this perilous journey cannot be guaranteed but he will *not* be travelling alone. His companions will be twelve dwarfs and their former king Thorin. Before they head out on their journey the conversation between Gandalf and Bilbo goes like this:

> Gandalf: "You'll have a tale or two to tell when you come back."
> Bilbo: "You will promise that I will come back?"
> Gandalf: "No and if you do, you'll not be the same."[112]

Life is a challenge to be lived but we do not need to travel alone! And if you choose to live it for Jesus the same promise will be made to you as Bilbo Baggins... *"if you do (live for Jesus) you will not be the same!"*

WHO CAN HELP?

You can receive guidance and assistance during the journey with help from above as you *"keep your eyes on Jesus"* (Hebrews 12:2 The Message). Depending on how you grew up, you might consider your parents and family members as reliable travelling partners. Friends (another chapter in the book) were especially important for accountability when I was in high school and beyond. Hopefully you have a church community whom you can also rely on in times of trouble.

I want to focus on one other category that was crucial for me growing up and now I get to give back in this area. It is the idea of having a mentor. Again from Hebrews 12 it says, *"Therefore, since we are surrounded by such a great cloud of witnesses..."* (Hebrews 12:1 NIV) I can clearly recall those mentors in my life who surrounded me with guidance, acceptance, and challenged me to grow.

Mr. W was a public high school counselor who invited me to go to a Christian camp, which became the beginning of my journey to Christ. Mr. W was prompted to find some young men and women, believers or not, and encourage them to go to camp. The person asking Mr. W to do this was Pete.

Pete, a Young Life leader, was new in the area and just looking for potential leaders for the future. He became the first person with whom I could have deep conversations about Christianity. Pete had a young and fiery leader named Bo.

Bo became the first youth pastor I worked under as a volunteer. Bo gave me so many opportunities to experiment with leadership and deepen my faith. Bo attended San Jose Bible College (later becoming San Jose Christian College and then William Jessup University where I teach now) and it was through him I met Bryce.

Bryce Jessup is a former President of WJU; an amazing and consistent man of God who hired me to work at the college. I've known Bryce now for about 40 years and I still chat with him often. I will always look up to him as the model for how I want to live my life and be remembered. Thanks Bryce!

I realized as I was reflecting on who God put in my life that these four men all mentored me in sequence to lead me to where I am even now!

WHAT IS A MENTOR?

A mentor is defined as *a trusted counselor or guide.* It is to give advice and instruction (to someone) regarding the course or process to be followed.[113]

In Greek mythology Mentor was a friend of Odysseus (the Greek King of Ithaca) who was entrusted with the education of Odysseus' son Telemachus. Mentor was older and wiser with some experiences behind him. A mentor is often older and wiser, but not always. Sometimes a mentor is just a good trusted friend!

> "Mentoring is a brain to pick, an ear to listen and a push in the right direction."
> John C. Crosby

Just as so many, if not almost all movies are about journeys or quests, many movies contain a relationship between a mentor and mentee. What about the movie you thought about earlier? Does it have this kind of relationship? Here are a few examples of powerful and well-known mentors in movies: *Karate Kid* (Mr. Miyagi), *Star Wars* (Yoda or Obi-Wan Kenobi), *Narnia* (Aslan),

Harry Potter (Professor Albus Dumbledore), *Lord of the Rings* (Gandalf) and this list could go on!

Our mentors help us keep going on the journey, to push past pain and the confusion of growing up, to get a right perspective on life. According to Hebrews 12, mentors help point out sin and other wrong things in our life, with love, so that we can correct them! This allows us to not get bogged down in life but learn to thrive!

RUNNING ALONE

I had the opportunity to run the San Francisco Half Marathon a few years back as a fundraiser for St. Jude's Children's Hospital. My son-in-law, Justin, and I took off fast zipping by people and cruising across the Golden Gate Bridge. After about ten miles (with three miles

> *"If I have seen further it is by standing on the shoulders of giants."*
> Isaac Newton

left to go) my young running partner took off leaving me to finish alone. All of a sudden I felt like I had cement running shoes.

Just as I was about ready to stop jogging and just walk the rest of the course, I heard the faint noise of people yelling. I wearily plodded around a corner and it was the home stretch of the half-marathon. All the spectators were cheering for runners, especially *me* since I was wearing a jersey that identified me as a Saint Jude's Hero running to raise money for kids with cancer! Immediately my feet felt as light as feathers and I starting sprinting toward the finish like an Olympic runner! I was exhausted but the energy of the crowd helped me run hard and finish strong!

Our life journey is ongoing and when we are exhausted or feel like we can't go on, we need those mentors to cheer us along towards the finish of the race.

THE CHALLENGE

The challenge for this chapter is potentially two-fold. The first part is finding a mentor, but who? Consider people who work in a field you would potentially like to work in someday. Perhaps someone who is wise and you would like to "be like" later in life. Someone who is older and has some experiences in life.

Simply approach them and ask them if they would consider mentoring you for a period of time. Spend a little time at the first meeting telling them more about you, your hopes and dreams, etc. Then go for it! You should share about things going on in your life but *the idea is to let the mentor speak into YOUR life* in these areas as well!

The second part of the challenge is being a mentor. You may not think YOU are ready to mentor someone; that you don't have what it takes or you are too young or (insert complaint here!). But you are ready! Remember Frodo Baggins didn't think he was ready either…

"I am not made for perilous quests. I wish I had never seen the Ring! Why did it come to me? Why was I chosen?'
'Such questions cannot be answered,' said Gandalf. 'You may be sure that it was not for any merit that others do not possess: not for power or wisdom, at any rate. But you have

been chosen, and you must therefore use such strength and heart and wits as you have."

You have been chosen. Simply keep your eyes open to those around you and use everything you have as you invest in others!

TO THINK ABOUT...
1. Have I ever HAD a true mentor? Who? Why do I consider them a mentor?

2. What qualities seemed most important to me in that kind of relationship?

3. Have I ever had the chance TO BE a mentor to a friend or someone younger than myself? Who? What did I do with that opportunity?

4. Is there a situation now where I either need a mentor or could be a mentor to someone?

Chapter 28

GET OVER YOURSELF

The Blessing of Serving Others

By Mary Ann McMillan

Did you know that when serving, the most important things you have to offer are *not* things, it is yourself? Reflect on that for a second. Many times we think that the best way to serve people is by giving them material things. In reality what they really need is a person to help them. Someone to come alongside them and love them.

When was the last time you served others? Where was it and what was involved? What does serving look like to you? If you are not currently serving somewhere, why not? What do you need to do in order to make time for others? Start thinking through those questions as you read through this chapter.

DYING TO SELF

Moving back to the United States after serving overseas for several years was the hardest thing I have ever done. I enjoyed my life away from the "American dream" and American culture. I got to blend in with the world and share the gospel with those who didn't know Jesus. Serving as a whole was so different. It was all about relationship building and loving people. I enjoyed the adventure.

"Home" in the United States of America should have felt normal, but it didn't. Nothing was the same. I had changed. My family and friends had changed. I had no clue how to be "normal" in a culture that was supposed to feel familiar. I questioned the Lord a lot during this time. What am I doing with my life? What will ministry look like in an "I have everything, I don't need to serve anyone" context? I struggled with being back. How could I serve and do ministry in a first world country when I didn't even want to be here?

For me, returning home felt like dying. This was not a physical death but a *dying to self* that I seemed to be fighting against as I worked to settle back into this life. I certainly did not feel this way on the mission field, but back home I believed I was entitled to certain rights; the right to have a home, new clothes, perfect friends, great ministry, to blend in, the perfect job, and for everyone to respect me. All I wanted was a perfect life! Yet the reality is that as a child of God none of those things are promised to me.

> To "take up our cross" means to treasure Jesus more than we treasure human approval, honor, comfort and life.

Through these struggles with feeling entitled, I contemplated what Jesus said to His disciples in Luke 9:23. *"If anyone would come after me, let him deny himself and take up his cross daily and follow me."* (ESV) Following Jesus means that we need to get over ourselves. We need to let go of the comforts we believe we deserve and be obedient to Him.

Another way to look at this is when Jesus said that the way to follow Him was to take up our cross, He meant we should be willing (without murmuring, or God-criticism, or cowardice) to be *opposed*, to be *shamed*, to *suffer*, and to *die* — all for our allegiance to Him. Or, to go to the heart of the matter, to "take up our cross" means to treasure Jesus more than we treasure human approval, honor, comfort, and life.[114] Our suffering is not a tribute to Jesus unless we endure it because we cherish Jesus.

NO EXCUSES

What holds us back from serving others? One answer is sin. Sin makes us self-centered, and many of us build our entire lives around getting what we want. Yet Jesus said the most important truths are to love God and love others.[115] This requires us to die to self and put ourselves last. Our lives are changed when we live according to God's Word in a self-sacrificial way. We no longer think about our selfish desires. We consider what others need first and how we can serve them.

Often it seems like we are waiting for the perfect conditions in order to serve. We use the excuse that we are too busy, we are having a rough time, or we have more important things to do with our time. The problem is, we will always be busy. If we wait for the perfect timing we will never get anything done. Those times when you feel like you shouldn't serve are the times that you should serve. In those times it's actually a great time to focus on others instead of turning inward and focusing on your own problems.

Another excuse might be, I don't have anything to offer. That's not true at all. We all have something to offer. You are needed. Don't leave it up to someone else to do the work you could be doing. Don't be intimidated. Just be yourself and serve. We are all called for a different purpose but those purposes are important. Wherever you are, God has something vital going on.

BENEFITS OF SERVING

One of the greatest benefits of serving is your ability to make a difference in the lives of others. It is no secret...we live in a dark and needy world and God has a plan for you in relation to this. Listen to how scripture lays this out for us, *"For we are his workmanship, created in Christ Jesus for good works, which God prepared beforehand, that we should walk in them."* (Ephesians 2:10 ESV) Do you see this? God has something prepared just for you!

> *Happiness can actually increase in our life when we are serving.*

Studies show that happiness can actually increase in our life when we are serving. A part of our brain lights up when we help others! It seems when we just focus inward we become self-obsessed and more depressed. Looking outward, and into the lives of others, can reduce our stress and even help us live longer.[116]

Other benefits of serving include learning how to be a part of a team (working to accomplish a single goal), using or trying out new skills and gifts, and teaching humility. Serving can even help you become a better employee in the future.[117]

If you are college age or a young adult you may use volunteering as a resume booster. Every church and organization needs volunteers in every corner of their business from marketing to social media to sales and grunt work. You can work in so many different areas to learn new skills. As a volunteer, you will be able to add this work to your resume.

When you become a valuable volunteer to an organization, you'll not only get the opportunity to network with the staff of the organization but often also the board (particularly if you volunteer during fundraising events), many of whom are business leaders outside of the non-profit space. You can make connections to powerful movers and shakers in the industry you plan to enter post-College.[118]

Having great references can be the key to success in landing that first job after college. If you become a volunteer for a church or organization, you will likely receive many great references that most churches and nonprofit team members will be happy to share with your prospective employers. Therefore, do well in these roles.

OK, LET'S SERVE!

What are some ways to get involved with serving? Always start with prayer. Before you make a decision to volunteer and serve, I suggest that you spend time in prayer. Pray for your heart, asking the Lord to help prepare you for serving. It is in prayer that we discern God's will for us and build spiritual dependence on the Lord. Prayer will also help prepare you for opportunities to share about Christ.

Although opportunities to serve are limitless, you can start in some very simple ways. Begin right where you are by being a good neighbor. Find ways to serve in your school or community. Tutor and teach children. This can be at your local schools, in the inner city, or even helping adults learn English as a second language. Serve at soup kitchens and homeless shelters. So many people are needed to pick up, prepare, serve and clean up after a meal to those coming for a food blessing! Visit a convalescent home to read or just sit and chat with the elderly. What else comes to mind?

THE CHALLENGE

What moves you? Who or what are you passionate about? Are you frustrated by any injustice around you? Explore these areas as somewhere you might want to serve. Contact the person or agency and find out what might be available. Then GO and serve! Remember you are needed and what you do matters.

TO THINK ABOUT...

1. As believers why is serving others important?

2. Do I believe that I can help someone? Why?

3. Why is prayer important when serving?

4. As I think about the world or just my community, what are ways I would like to serve?

Chapter 29

SURPRISED BY JOY

Delighting in Life

By Erin Hill

How often do you feel joy? What makes you feel joyful? What are you doing when you experience joy? Are you sharing time with family or friends? Are you relaxing with a good book? Are you listening to your favorite music? Take a few moments to consider these important questions.

Here are a few more questions: How much joy do you experience on a daily basis? Do you add joyful experiences into your schedule? Do

> "We cannot cure the world of sorrows, but we can choose to live in joy." Joseph Campbell

you think most people have a hard time experiencing joy? If so, why?

WHAT IS JOY?

The word 'joy' is defined as "the emotion evoked by well-being, success, or good fortune or by the prospect of possessing what one desires...the expression or exhibition of such emotion...a state of happiness." [119] What are the things that provide you with well-being, success, good fortune, and the feeling of happiness? Most people include relationships, job satisfaction, and wealth as sources of joy.

Catherine Sanderson, a psychology professor at Amherst College, gave a talk titled *Positive Psychology: The Science of Happiness*, in which she described things that we think will make us happy but don't, and things that really do. One of the items that truly brings people happiness is faith. Religious beliefs, she says, "give people a sense of meaning." It also gives them a social network. "It gives a sense of well-being or comfort."[120]

Additional research supports this idea of social connection and the support that religion offers. According to a study published in the journal *American Sociological Review*, religious people gain life satisfaction

> "Find out where joy resides, and give it a voice far beyond singing. For to miss the joy is to miss all."
> Robert Louis Stevenson

thanks to social networks they build by attending religious services. The surveys showed that across all creeds, religious people were more satisfied than non-religious people. According to the data, about 28 percent of people who attended a religious service weekly were "extremely satisfied" with their lives, compared with 19.6 percent of people who never attended services.[121]

The experts agree a sense of happiness is achieved when we connect with other people. Attending church and connecting with other individuals helps offer this positive connection. When we are at church we are automatically surrounded with others who have something in common with us; worshiping the same God.

It is a catalyst for relationship and offers the opportunity to get to know other individuals at a greater level.

I feel an instant connection with other believers, even at a church that I've never attended before. How can I explain this feeling? It's an automatic sense of belonging when I walk in the doors of the church. I know those around me believe in the same God that I do. It is important to share our faith with others because it helps relieve feelings of loneliness and isolation that can result from a lack of fellowship with others.

SURPRISED BY JOY

The phrase surprised by joy comes from C.S. Lewis' book *by the same name*, which is a spiritual biography about the nature of joy. His work played a leading role in his exploration from atheism to Christianity. It further represents those factors that brought Lewis to a mature, adult Christian faith. In his book, Lewis expanded the concept of joy to "capture and explain his inner longings for God that are universally experienced." He concluded that the reconnection to God and a glimpse of what is eternal exceeded everything else in life.[122]

C.S. Lewis explored his faith and established that the *connection with God is a key to joy*. He further discusses friendship as a chief source of happiness. The experts agree that close friendships and connection to God is a pathway to joy.

There will be a few questions to consider at the end of the chapter but take a moment to reflect on these thoughts now. Have you ever been surprised by joy?

What were the circumstances? What was it about the situation that brought you joy? If Lewis is right then perhaps we all have an inner longing for God. Has your relationship with God been a pathway to joy? What does that look like for you?

Here's what joy looks like for me. Others refer to me joyful and say that I inspire them. This is not something that I try to do or be. After reflecting on how I maintain a joyful approach to life, I believe that I can sum it up in a few words. *I seek joy.* I actively pursue joy every day. Why do I do this? I grew up taking care of my paralyzed father who was sick for over 20 years. I grew up in a challenging environment where I could have been perpetually sad but I chose joy. I chose to thank God that I could spend time with my dad on a daily basis. I actively pursued the good things that were happening in the midst of tragedy. That's why my foundational verse is Nehemiah 8:10 *"The joy of the Lord is my strength"* because it really is.

WHAT DOES THE BIBLE SAY ABOUT JOY?

Although joy can be experienced through our faith, attending church, and a connection with others; it can also be experienced through Scripture. Read these verses slowly as you ponder God's joy in your life.

"Many people say, 'Who will show us better times?' Let you face smile on us, Lord. You have given me greater joy than those who have abundant harvests of grain and new wine." (Psalm 4:6-7 NLT)

"But the Holy Spirit produces this kind of fruit in our lives: love, joy, peace, patience, kindness, goodness, faithfulness, gentleness, and self-control." (Galatians 5:22-23a NLT)

"Always be full of joy in the Lord. I say it again-rejoice!" (Philippians 4:4 NLT)

"A joyful heart is good medicine, but a broken spirit dries up the bones." (Proverbs 17:22 NASB)

DISCOVER YOUR JOY

What is the solution to a lack of joy? What can we do on a day-to-day basis to help us achieve joy? Here are a few ideas: discover your joy by taking a joy quiz, writing out your joy-list, or experiencing an activity that makes you happy.

Joy Quiz

Do you like to take fun, non-academic quizzes? Try taking a Joy Quiz and discover where you are on the joy meter. The Berkeley Well Being Institute Quiz is one option.[123]

Write Your Joy-List

Create a specific list that includes ten or more things that truly bring you joy. For a greater challenge expand your list to twenty-five or fifty items!

Experience a Joyful Activity

Volunteer – Think about the skills that you enjoy sharing and volunteer at your favorite organization.

Donate – Donate your excess goods that don't bring you joy but could help someone else.

Be Active – Take a walk, go for a run, set out on a hike, or ride your bike around the neighborhood.

Relax – Sit outside, smell the roses, listen to music, or watch the sunrise/sunset.

THE CHALLENGE

Consider intentionally experiencing joy as soon as possible. Review the ideas list above and challenge yourself to participate in one of them. Finally, don't be shy about sharing your joy with others, you never know who needs your infectious attitude. You can do this!

I'm thanking you, God, from a full heart,
I'm writing the book on your wonders.
I'm whistling, laughing, and jumping for joy;
I'm singing your song, High God.
(Psalm 9:1-2 The Message)

TO THINK ABOUT...

1. How is my current joy meter (empty, full, or somewhere in between)?

2. How can choosing joy help my life improve?

3. Can I create a joy experience? Which one? When should I start?

4. Is there something else I should explore on this topic?

Chapter 30

AN ATTITUDE OF GRATITUDE

The Impact of Practicing Thankfulness

By Dawn Pickering

How would you like to have the opportunity to be 25 percent happier, more energetic, and experience deeper connections in your relationships?[124] Do you desire to feel more inspired, reduce negative stress, and enjoy improved health?[125] Research shows that all of this can be true for you, *if* you are willing to practice gratitude. Let's unpack this appealing topic and explore gratitude, its benefits, and how to practice it.

WHAT IS GRATITUDE?

Gratitude involves first recognizing that we have benefited from a circumstance or another person's kindness and generosity. Gratitude begins with awareness, which in turn fuels feelings of appreciation. This feeling may then be followed by verbalizing our thankfulness. Other terms for gratitude include thankfulness, appreciation, recognition, and acknowledgement. Practicing gratitude is powerful. It changes a person's life because it changes the person. Gratitude can even be considered worship because expressing appreciation to God is an act of thankfulness, worship, and praise.

THE BENEFITS OF GRATITUDE

Studies by Dr. Robert Emmons, a world leader in gratitude research, reveal the benefits of practicing gratitude. His research reports that recognizing and acknowledging benefits in our lives aids in blocking toxic emotions such as envy, resentment, regret, and depression.[126]

Another benefit of gratitude is that it grows peace in one's mind and heart; it cultivates contentment. When we pause to recognize good that comes from outside ourselves, our focus is placed on people and things worth

> One benefit of gratitude is that it cultivates contentment.

celebrating. We start paying attention to the positives rather than setting up camp in the wilderness of negatives and "what ifs." Our mind cannot focus on gratitude and complain at the same time, so the choice to focus our mind on gratitude pushes out lingering and unwelcome negative thoughts. Pausing and looking at nature or recognizing a kind gesture can invoke feelings of gratitude. It can be a beautiful sunset, finding a shady place to rest on a warm day, a smile, or a thoughtful word. Each of these, and so many more moments, provide opportunities to feel thankful if we recognize them.

An additional benefit to the practice of gratitude is that it pleases God. 1 Thessalonians 5:18 instructs us to *"Be thankful in all circumstances, for this is God's will for you who belong to Christ Jesus."* (NLT) Many people misunderstand this verse and think they have to be thankful *for* their circumstance, but let's take a closer look.

It says *in* your circumstances, not *for* them. In the midst of difficult times we can find and focus on things for which we can be thankful. Even in the midst of grief and sorrow over the passing of a loved one, we can be grateful to have had someone so special in our life.

Gratitude can be a bit of a treasure hunt because sometimes it takes some searching. When I was eight months pregnant a woman ran a red light and broadsided my Suburban. I sustained multiple injuries and went into active labor that continued for six weeks. By God's sweet grace, my mom arrived at the scene of the accident within 60 seconds of it happening, providing help and comfort. My two young sons were both buckled safely in center seats protecting them from injury, and in spite of the trauma and lengthy labor, I gave birth to a healthy baby boy. Even in the midst of a very difficult situation the foundation of my trust in God enabled me to recognize these treasures.

Despite present circumstances, one can always be thankful. Paul writes to the church at Philippi, *"Don't worry about anything; instead, pray about everything. Tell God what you need and thank him for all he has done."* (Philippians 4:6 NLT) In our difficult times we have a powerful and caring heavenly Father who wants us to bring our concerns to Him, and in doing so we can approach Him with gratitude for His loving care for us. A welcome benefit is peace of heart and mind.

Practicing gratitude will enhance our relationship with God because when we thank Him, we focus on acknowledging who He is and all that He has done and continues to do. We can always be thankful that through Jesus, God saved us from the deserved penalty of our sin, restoring our relationship with Him.[127] We can also be grateful for His ongoing work in our lives that enables us to mature spiritually.[128] Even in the most difficult season of life we can be thankful that God's love cannot be taken from us.[129]

Practicing gratitude can actually reshape *our* attitude. For an attitude to develop it needs to be nurtured and fed. As a reminder about the importance of attitude, Chuck Swindoll composed the following piece of wisdom.

> The longer I live, the more I realize the impact of attitude on life. Attitude, to me, is more important than the past, than education, than money, than circumstances, than failures, than success, than what other people think or say or do. It is more important than appearance, giftedness or skill. It will make or break an organization...a school...a home.
> The remarkable thing is we have a choice every day regarding the attitude we will embrace for that day. We cannot change our past. We cannot change the fact that people will act in a certain way. We cannot change the inevitable. The only thing we can do is play on the one string we have – and that is our attitude. I am convinced that life is 10 percent what happens to me and 90 percent how I react to it.[130]

Practicing gratitude reshapes our attitude because it affects how we see the world. It does not deny reality; it changes how we approach it. Our circumstances may not change but our perspective does. A wonderful outcome of practicing gratitude is that it actually begins to take less effort and happen more naturally, becoming a part of who we are...a grateful person.

HOW DO I START?

Imagine a world where everyone chose to practice and nurture gratitude in their lives. An attitude of entitlement would not exist, selfish attitudes would decline, and humans would act kindly and graciously with each other. Reality reminds us that this may never happen, but we can improve our own lives and impact our personal sphere of influence in a significant way. Becoming a person of gratitude begins with an *intentional choice* to focus our thoughts on what we have for which we can be thankful. It can be as ordinary as a bed, a place to live, enough food, or as significant as God's extravagant love for us.

Do you remember that inspired, happier, less-stressed, motivated, more energetic person with deeper relationship connections we talked about at the beginning of this chapter? Do you want that to describe you? Make the decision to take a step right now toward a healthier and happier you by practicing some gratitude. Your life will be better, and so will the lives of those in your circle of influence.

THE CHALLENGE

Consider the following list and choose one or more to begin to live a life of thankfulness.

Keep a gratitude journal or jar. At least every other day write down several things and/or people for whom you are grateful. Be specific and detailed. Keep it fresh by trying to include events that were unexpected (a nice surprise). Every so often read what you have written. There are also apps available for gratitude journaling, such as "Grateful: A Gratitude Journal".

Write a gratitude letter or make a gratitude visit. Think of someone that you appreciate. Tell them why you are grateful for them. Remember to be specific and detailed.

> *"Feeling gratitude and not expressing it is like wrapping a present and not giving it."*
> William Arthur Ward

Choose to read a blog, article, or book about gratitude to inspire you to action. I highly recommend, *Gratitude Works!* as an informative resource for practicing gratitude.

Consider an area of difficulty in your life right now. List what you can be grateful for in spite of this circumstance. Whenever you focus on the difficulty in a way that is unproductive, read your gratitude list. Refocus your thoughts and grow an attitude of gratitude.

TO THINK ABOUT...

1. What specifically about this chapter stood out to me?

2. Would I describe myself as a grateful person? If not what is preventing me from being thankful?

3. What is *one thing* I am grateful for right now?

4. Which of the challenges from above do I need to incorporate into my life today?

Chapter 31

LIGHTEN UP

Learning to Laugh & Play More Often

By Fritz Moga

What a fantastic weekend I just had! It was my birthday weekend and I had one of those "treat yo self" kind of weekends![131] I started the first day with an enthusiastic yoga class (yes yoga). Following that, I sat outside at a favorite bakery and overindulged in a cinnamon roll with copious amounts of frosting (sort of the yin/yang of exercise and eating). The weekend went on to include a long bike ride, time outside doing yardwork, going

> *What would be on your list for a perfect, fun weekend?*

out for a couple meals with family members, watching a few movies on Netflix, and of course going to church! Phew, makes me tired just thinking about it but it was so much fun.

Well at least it was fun for me, but what about you? What would be on your list for the perfect, *fun* weekend? Take a minute and jot down some of the things you really enjoy, that settle you down or amp you up. List those things that are just straight out fun for you!

LAUGHING IS CRUCIAL

Since this book has been about stress, busyness, anxiety and the like, we need to mention something that releases our emotions in a fun and silly way...laughter! Here are some fun facts and figures about laughter: • On average, a child laughs 300 times a day while an adult laughs only 17 times a day. • The majority of men report that their laughter is a chuckle, and the majority of women report that theirs is a giggle. • Adults between the ages of 18 and 34 report laughing the most. • Most laughter does not come from listening to jokes; it comes from spending time with family and friends. • People tend to laugh more when in groups. People should surround themselves with others who laugh, because laughter is contagious. • Smiling is a mild, silent form of laughing. • Babies start to laugh at about four months of age.[132]

Smiling, giggling, chuckle. How many names are there for laughing? Turns out quite a few. Here a few more to chortle at...belly laugh, bray, cachinnation, cackle, guffaw, hew-haw, shriek, crack-up, convulse, howl, roar, snicker, and snort. You can be in fits, in hysterics or in stitches. You might almost wet yourself, lose it, split your sides or die laughing! Who knew?

THE BEST MEDICINE?
It is hard to say where "laughter is the best medicine" originated but some postulate it might be from the Bible, specifically Proverbs.

"A cheerful heart is good medicine, but a crushed spirit dries up the bones." (Proverbs 17:22 NIV)

The Bible has consistently shown us what doctors continually try to prove true though research. In this case, studies show us that laughing and having a happy heart is good for our health. One writer shares the fact we know laughter is one of the best tools for dealing with stress but says "Research into laughter goes even further, revealing that it's a potent drug with the contagious power of a virus that conveys a slew of benefits for the mind and body."[133] Here are a few interesting health related results of laughing.

Laughing brings people together. It is more than just attending a party or having a few friends over for dinner. Laughter releases endorphins, a feel-good chemical in the brain. So when you gather together, someone shares a funny story and the laughter begins, you feel good and it enhances the social bond you have with others.

Laughter is a key to relationships. Men and women both rate a sense of humor as a top tier trait for a potential partner. Couples who laugh together report having a higher quality relationship than those who don't spend time laughing.[134]

When you laugh it boosts the immune system. Want to stay healthy? Laugh more often. Laughter decreases stress hormones and increases immune cells and infection-fighting antibodies, thus improving your resistance to disease.[135]

Laughing burns calories. According to a Vanderbilt University study, just ten to fifteen minutes of laughing a day can burn up to 40 calories, which can translate to actually losing three or four pounds over the course of a year.[136]

Simply laughing more often can reduce anxiety, improve your cardiovascular system, may reduce your blood pressure, temporarily relieve pain, and one more…laughter may even help you to live longer.[137] Although it's just two names, famous comedians Bob Hope and George Burns both lived to be 100!

> *Laughing burns calories, can reduce anxiety, and may even help you live longer!*

Go for it. Hangout with some friends, find the humor in life, go on social media and watch people fall down, binge watch an entire season of your favorite sitcom. With these simple steps you may reduce stress and live longer!

TAKING PLAYTIME SERIOUSLY

As a child your well-meaning but frustrated mom may have told you "go outside and play" but it really wasn't punishment was it? Play was a core aspect of being a child. Playing with dolls, creating stories and acting them out, riding a bike, climbing a tree or reading a book for fun was all part of a normal life.

Myriads of studies confirm the positive cognitive and social development issues surrounding playtime as children; but should it stop there? What about us adults? Do we get to play too? *What if* (now stick with me here for a moment), *what if* adults got recess? How great would that be? Imagine for a moment it's 10am on a workday. Yes it's break time but instead of that cigarette out on the loading dock or that brisk ten minute walk, you got the chance to play. I'm talking nerf guns, swings, maybe an intense game of tag, and the *piece de resistance* – a bouncy house! The rest of the day would probably include some laughter recalling stories such as when "so-and-so" fell down during duck, duck goose. It might also generate a more positive attitude toward work in general (but perhaps we'll need to bring back nap time as well).

We live in a play-deprived culture. When "adulting" kicks in during the late college years, so much is expected from you at work and in life. You need to be successful, have a family, go to Hawaii every year for vacation (yea, I see it on Facebook all the time) and to plan for your future. We strive for perfection, we persevere in life yet we need to add we play for health and happiness.

Play will look different for everyone. Dr. Stuart Brown from the National Institute for Play (I know where I want my next job to be) says; "Play is something done for its own sake, it's voluntary, it's pleasurable, it offers a sense of

> "You can discover more about a person in an hour of play than in a year of conversation." Plato

engagement, it take you out of time. And the act itself is more important than the outcome."[138]

I once heard this quote and it's stuck with me; "Growing older is mandatory, growing *up* is optional!" So what's your pleasure? Consider the following as you begin to build your list of playtime options. Run through a grassy field. Jump on a swing and see how high you can go. Throw a water-balloon at someone. Collect stamps. Play the guitar. Toss around a Frisbee. Go to the ocean and squish your toes into the wet sand. Act out charades with friends. Play dress-up with some children.

Shoot some hoops. Write a limerick. Watch the History Channel. Just act silly for a few minutes!

DID THEY LAUGH & PLAY IN THE BIBLE?

Ecclesiastes makes it clear there is *"a time to weep and a time to laugh, a time to mourn and a time to dance."* (Ecclesiastes 3:4 NIV) God actually laughs (Psalm 22:4; 37:12-13) and he delights in YOU and will rejoice over you with singing (Zephaniah 3:17). There were many festivals and celebrations in the ancient world, which I must assume

> *Growing older is mandatory, growing up is optional.*

would include laughing, dancing, and a playful spirit! There is so much more to be said about this topic but let's suffice it to say since we are created in God's image, we too can laugh, and sing, and play.

THE CHALLENGE

This is the final, and therefore the most important, challenge of this book (read this in a not very serious voice please). Did you make a list of the things you do for fun? Then DO IT! Be intentional in creating space for play in your life. Surround yourself with *fun* people with whom you can enjoy life together. Laugh and play. Don't take life so seriously. YOU GOT THIS!

TO THINK ABOUT...

1. What is the last thing I did for crazy fun?

2. What makes me laugh or just feel happy?

3. What seems to prevent me from laughing or taking time to play?

4. How can I actually create space (plan, prioritize, schedule) for some play time?

CONTRIBUTING AUTHORS' BIOS

<u>Erin Ambrose, PhD</u>
Erin Ambrose is an Associate Professor of Psychology at William Jessup University and a Licensed Marriage and Family Therapist, with a private practice in Roseville, CA. With over twenty years of experience working in mental health, she is passionate about helping people live productive and satisfying lives. When not in the classroom or seeing clients, you will often find Erin running, hiking, or chasing her beagle!

<u>Matt Bach, MA</u>
Matt has served professionally in ministry for over 17 years in both NorCal, SoCal, and New Zealand. He currently functions as the Pastor of Christian Development at Bridgeway Christian Church in Roseville, CA overseeing all classes, research, education, and equipping. He teaches Hebrew Bible/Old Testament Survey as well as Youth Culture, Trends and Issues as an adjunct faculty at William Jessup University. In addition to leading study tours to Israel, he just began Ph.D. work in Biblical Studies in England. Matt enjoys time with his wife and three kids, nerding out on everything Tolkien, Star Wars or the Bible.

<u>Steve Backers, B.S.C Finance; MBA</u>
Prior to William Jessup University, Steve had a distinguished corporate career of over 25 years in Finance, Human Resources, and Operations at Intel Corporation. He left Intel to help launch a health technology start-up where he was Human Resources Director, then Chief Financial Officer (CFO) and Chief Operating Officer (COO). Steve then became COO of a Sacramento area non-profit, Saint John's Program for Real Change. He is now an Assistant Professor in the School of Business. In the community, Steve serves as

Chairman of the Board for an area non-profit, Hands4Hope – Youth Making a Difference.

Libby Backfish, PhD
Libby is an assistant professor of Old Testament at William Jessup University. She loves teaching and researching a broad range of topics pertinent to the Old Testament, but her areas of specialty include Hebrew poetry, Old Testament theology, the book of Psalms, and textual criticism. Libby stays busy adventuring with her family: skiing, rock climbing, riding bikes, and otherwise exploring beautiful northern California. She and her family make their home in Roseville, CA, and they are active members of Granite Springs Church in Lincoln, CA.

Kristen Crichton, LMFT
Adjunct Professor Kristen Crichton has been teaching in the Psychology Department at WJU since 2005. She is a Licensed Marriage and Family Therapist with a private practice in Fair Oaks, CA where she helps individuals and families heal from all the trials that life brings. She enjoys speaking at local churches to help strengthen and encourage people in the joys and challenges of marriage and raising kids. Kristen enjoys spending time with her husband and their blended family. When she has time, Kristen cherishes moments to go for a run or hop on her bike for a quiet ride along the river.

Parker Daniells, MS
Assistant Professor Parker Daniells serves as lead faculty for the Kinesiology program. Parker has been at William Jessup University since 2009 as a coach for Cross Country and Track & Field before becoming a professor in 2017. Parker enjoys serving the local running community of Placer and Sacramento County by coaching and putting on races. During the school year, you will see Parker with

the Cross Country and Track & Field teams serving as an Assistant Coach in the distance events. When Parker is not in the classroom or at the track, he is outside fishing, backpacking, surfing, and kayaking with his family.

Thomas Fitzpatrick, MS
Thomas is the campus pastor at William Jessup University. He has been doing college ministry for over 13 years at his Alma Mater, The University of New Mexico, as well as at Pepperdine University in Malibu, CA. Thomas also served as the lead pastor at West Bowles Community Church in Littleton, CO. Besides ministering to college students and helping them become more like Jesus, Thomas loves preaching, snowboarding, woodworking, and all things golf. His main love is his family, which is comprised of his beautiful wife, Becca, and his three precious girls.

Daniel Gluck, PhD
Daniel Gluck serves as Associate Professor and Associate Dean for Jessup's School of Christian Leadership. He has served in higher education for most of his career, and joined Jessup in 2004 as Director of Campus Ministries. Daniel holds a Ph.D. in Organizational Leadership from Eastern University in Pennsylvania. He is passionate about spiritual formation, global outreach, and leadership development. He has traveled to over 30 countries, and works with a number of nonprofits globally. Daniel loves experiencing new cultures, playing guitar, enjoying the outdoors and going on adventures with his wife Alyssa, and three amazing kids.

Matthew Godshall, PhD
Matt joined the Faculty of Theology of William Jessup University in the spring on 2015 and is an Associate Professor of New Testament and Theology. He serves as the Lead Faculty for the Theology program and is a

committee member of the Institute for Biodiversity and the Environment. Matt teaches a variety of New Testament and Theology courses and has a passion for helping students understand, love and enter into the biblical story. Matt also seeks to serve his church through occasional preaching, participating in the worship ministry and as a member of the Leadership Team.

Laura Hall, PhD, RDN
Laura graduated from Cal Poly, San Luis Obispo with her Bachelors in Nutrition. She then attended the dietetic internship at UCSF Medical Center where she became a Registered Dietitian Nutritionist (RDN). Laura received her PhD from UC Davis in Nutritional Biology with an emphasis in International and Community Nutrition. She worked as an Assistant Professor at Cal Poly and as a Clinical Dietitian. Laura has taught nutrition at several different community colleges and William Jessup University. She is also working on starting a Nutrition Program at WJU. She enjoys teaching students about health and wellness. She's a busy mom with 3 kids who loves hiking/running and making healthy meals for her family.

Dave Heitman, MA
Dave is originally from California and has studied and worked in over 25 countries, most recently as a church planter for 7 years in New Zealand. In addition to being a pastor, Dave has worked in Christian higher education since 2001 and is finishing his doctorate in Education and Organizational Leadership at University of the Pacific. Dave serves as the current Dean of Students at William Jessup University. Dave loves his wife Melissa and their four children Noah, Corban, Hope, and Halee, as well as being outdoors, surfing, snowboarding, of course, Jesus and His church.

Emily Hill, MFA

Emily Hill serves as Adjunct Faculty in the Visual and Fine Arts Department. She has been at William Jessup University since 2012 when she started as an undergraduate student in the brand new Creative Arts department! After completing her MFA in Writing for Children and Young Adults, she was thrilled to return to teach at Jessup. Emily loves combining her faith and passion for visual and written arts in classes like Storytelling for Multimedia and The Creative Christian. When Emily isn't teaching she is often found writing, painting, or exploring a new creative medium.

Erin Hill, JD

Erin has been part of the Jessup family since 2014. Prior to Jessup, Erin spent several decades in positions such as business owner, attorney, and Vice President of Finance. Erin is an active Bible study leader, Sunday school teacher, and Worship leader at local churches. She delights in watching her students discover their joy and share it with others.

Christy Jewell, Director of Career & Life Planning

Christy has worked for William Jessup since 2004 where she shared the responsibility of raising support for student scholarships, communications and community outreach for the University for seven years, and has led the University's career development efforts since 2011. She now enjoys combining her community relations efforts with support of local business and organizations to find quality interns and employees. Christy completed her B.A. in Sociology at Westmont College, and is a certified Career Development Facilitator. She balances work and family life as a mom to two sons and wife to a police captain.

Kay Llovio, EdD

Passionate about Christian higher education and the transformation that takes place in students' lives, Dr. Kay Llovio was appointed Chief Student Life Officer at William Jessup University in 2013. She has been a member of the faculty at Jessup since 1985, serving first as the University Librarian and as professor of practical theology and education since 1990. Llovio's research interests include spirituality in higher education and the centrality of belief systems to an expression of personal leadership style. She has published in the *Christian Education Journal, Applied Anthropologist,* and *the Evangelical Dictionary of Christian Education.*

Meghan McMahon Johnson, MFTi, DM

Meghan McMahon Johnson hails from the bay area where she grew enjoying the soulful nature and atmosphere in Oakland Ca. Her education and love of sports led her to Sacramento CA where she completed her Bachelor's degree in Psychology, Master of Science degree in Counseling with an emphasis in Marriage, Family and Child Therapy, and lastly her Doctor of Management degree in Organizational Leadership. Her experience as a language and behavior therapist to children with autism, High School Counselor, SR. admissions representative and current Director of Student Care have fed her desire to help people see the best in themselves and equip them with the appropriate tools to succeed in life.

Mary Ann McMillian, EdD

Mary Ann serves as the Assistant Director of Campus Ministries. She is originally from Georgia and has a heart for reaching the nations. She has served in ministry for 13 years and has part of that period as a full time missionary with the International Mission Board. She is an advocate for vulnerable children and racial equality. In her free time, you can find her outdoors or in a coffee house drinking tea with friends.

Fritz Moga, MA

Associate Professor Fritz serves as the lead faculty for the Youth Ministry degree program. He has been at William Jessup University since 2000 when it was still San Jose Christian College! He served as Director of Campus Ministries for four years before becoming a professor. Fritz loves leading missions and educational trips around the globe and currently serves on a board for a ministry in Brazil. When Fritz isn't teaching he is outside as an avid hiker and bicyclist or just enjoying the sun on his back as he is doing yardwork!

Mark Moore, PhD

Mark is an associate professor of theology and has been teaching at William Jessup University since 2010. He is also one of the hosts of Jessup's very first podcast: Jessup Think. Along with teaching, Mark serves as the Spiritual Formation Pastor for Faith Legacy Church in Sacramento. In his free time Mark enjoys playing soccer and collecting vintage stereo systems.

Ryan Murphy, MA

Ryan began teaching as an adjunct professor at William Jessup shortly after receiving his MA in Theology from Fuller Seminary's Sacramento campus. He loves having one foot in the church as a Youth Pastor at the Rock of Roseville, and one foot in the academy as he pursues his PhD at St. Mary's University in London. His passion in both is discipleship: he loves training up young leaders in the church while simultaneously studying the concept in early Christianity. He and his wife Morgan live in community with other young adults actively seeking to live on mission in Roseville where they also enjoy cooking, reading, and watching British crime dramas.

Michael Obermire, MBA

Michael is passionate about teaching, learning, growing in Christ and helping others to find and cultivate their Christ given passion. Prior to joining WJU, Michael spent 34 years in the manufacturing industry, leading the sales, marketing, planning, and supply chain functions as an executive in several California businesses. Michael began teaching in 2012 at CSU, Sacramento in their Executive MBA program. He joined WJU in 2016 teaching in their undergraduate and MBA programs. Michael received a BS in Industrial Engineering from CSU, Fresno, and an MBA from CSU, Sacramento. He is married, with three children and four grandchildren, and lives in Rocklin.

Dawn Pickering, MACM

Adjunct Professor Dawn Pickering teaches in the Division of Theology. She has served as a professional Christian educator for over 25 years. Following the teachings of Jesus and living well relationally are her passions. Dawn enjoys speaking at Women's events and Retreats and investing in people by encouraging them to build their lives based on biblical truths. She and her husband co-lead discipleship small group experiences in their home, nurturing practical spiritual growth. Her favorite past times include time with family, enjoying nature, and playing the board game Catan.

Mandy Schmidt

Mandy Schmidt serves as the Campus Ministries Coordinator at William Jessup University. A WJU alumna, she double majored in Bible and Theology and Psychology during her undergraduate time. She is currently pursuing a Master's in Counseling Psychology. Mandy loves connecting with and encouraging others in their faith. When she isn't busy with work or school, she loves to spend her free time laughing with friends, reading fiction, baking the world's best chocolate-chip cookies, or hanging out with her husband and dog.

Melanie Trowbridge, MD

Melanie gives credit to her undergraduate Christian education where there existed an intentionality and discipleship of the mind, taught by educators who had first learned this for themselves and were passing it on to the next generation. This foundation was the scaffolding for her further post graduate education in medicine and life-long learning as a child/adolescent/adult psychiatrist and university professor. Melanie enjoys equipping, encouraging, and educating others. Her passion is her family, spending time boon docking in 1964 Airstream, backpacking anywhere, and caring for a dozen acres of foothill earth that they and their animals call home.

Derek Zahnd, PhD

Derek teaches Bible, Theology, Ministry and Leadership classes at William Jessup University. He has served as a part-time youth worker, cross-cultural church planter, associate pastor, interim pastor and senior pastor. He has ministered in nine countries including Mexico, where he lived with his family for ten years. His research interests include Globalization, Ecclesiology and Leadership.

ENDNOTES

Introduction

[1]https://adaa.org/living-withanxiety/children/childhood-anxiety-disorders. Accessed January 12, 2019.

[2]https://adaa.org/about-adaa/press-room/facts-statistics. Accessed January 12 2019

[3]https://adaa.org/about-adaa/press-room/facts-statistics

[4]Timothy Gombis. (2010) *Drama of Ephesians.* Downers Grove: IVP Academic, pp68-69.

[5]https://twitter.com/henrinouwen/status/923520684378198016?lang=en. Accessed on May 13, 2019.

Chapter 2 – Spiritual Muscles

[6]The National Wellness Institute, which includes spirituality as one of six dimensions of wellness, notes that a healthy person lives a life that is consistent with their values and beliefs.

[7]Willard, Dallas. (1988) *The Spirit of the Disciplines: Understanding How God changes Lives.* New York: HarperCollins.

[8]Research has proven that Jordan is categorically greater than LeBron James and therefore the greatest basketball player of all time.

[9]Nouwen, Henri. (1994) *Here and Now: Living in the Spirit.* New York: Crossroad Publishing, p101.

[10]Foster, Richard. (1978) *Celebration of Discipline: The Path to Spiritual Growth.* New York: Harper & Row.

[11]The lists here are not exhaustive but serve as a good starting place.

Chapter 3 – Upwards

[12]Synnott, Mark. (2019) *Solo.* National Geographic, February 2019, 42-53. Throughout this chapter, references to Honnold's ascents of El Capitan come from Synnott's article.

[13]Ortberg, John. (2014) *Soul Keeping: Caring For the Most Important Part of You.* Grand Rapids, MI: Zondervan.

[14]For an introduction to a variety of spiritual pathways check out Gary Thomas (2010) *Sacred Pathways: Discover Your Soul's Path to God.* Grand Rapids, MI: Zondervan.

[15]The Barna Group. (2016) *Barna Trends 2017*. Grand Rapids, MI: Baker Books, p140.

[16]Strauss, Mark L., in Duvall, J. Scott and Hays, J. Daniel. (2012) *Grasping God's Word: A Hands-on Approach to Reading Interpreting and Applying the Bible*. Grand Rapids, MI: Zondervan, p11.

[17]Vanhoozer, Kevin J. in Duvall, J. Scott and Hays, J. Daniel. (2012). *Grasping God's Word: A Hands-on Approach to Reading Interpreting and Applying the Bible.* Grand Rapids, MI: Zondervan, p10.

[18]https://www.navigators.org/resource/topical-memory-system/. Accessed May 10, 2019.

Chapter 4 – Turn Down the Volume

[19]Hammer, M. S., Swinburn, T. K., & Neitzel, R. L. (2013) *Environmental noise pollution in the United States: developing an effectivepublichealthresponse.* https://www.ncbi.nlm.nih.gov/pmc/articles/PMC3915267/. Accessed May 14, 2019.

[20]Torgue, H., Paquette, D., Augoyard, J. F., MacCartney, A., & Canadian Electronic Library (Firm). (2006) *Sonic Experience: A Guide to Everyday Sounds.* Montreal [Que.]: MQUP, p13. Accessed May 14, 2019.

[21]Ibid, p. xv.

[22]http://www.dwillard.org/articles/individual/how-does-the-disciple-live. Accessed May 14, 2019.

[23]This is a summary of the work by Gregory O. Johnson in his PhD dissertation, *From Morning Watch to Quiet Time: The Historical and Theological Development of Private Prayer in Anglo-American Protestant Instruction,* 1870-1950. (2007) Saint Louis University, ProQuest Dissertations Publishing. Accessed May 14, 2019.

Chapter 5 – I Can Relate

[24]Dalmas Taylor & Irwin Altman. (1987) *Communication in interpersonal relationships: Social penetration processes.* In M. Roloff & G. Miller (Eds.), *Interpersonal processes: New directions in communication research* (pp. 257-277). Newbury Park, CA: Sage.

[25]Richard W. Kropf, Faith: Security and risk, New York: Paulist Press, 1990, 27.

[26]Chariots of Fire (movie). https://en.wikipedia.org/wiki/Chariots_of_Fire. Accessed May 19, 2019.

[27]Thomas, Gary. (2010) *Sacred Pathways: Discover your soul's path to God*. Grand Rapids: Zondervan, p23.

[28]Ibid, p152.

[29]Another resource is *Sacred Pathways: How do you connect with God?* by Chi Alpha Campus Ministries. Broken into two parts, the first part is an assessment that you can take to find out by which pathways you most easily connect with God. The second section describes each of the nine Sacred Pathways.

Chapter 6 – Don't Worry-Be Happy

[30]https://en.wikipedia.org/wiki/Alfred_E._Neuman. Accessed March 29, 2019.

[31]http://therussler.tripod.com/qq/neumanisms.html. Accessed March 29, 2019.

[32]*The Economic Burden of Anxiety Disorders*. A study commissioned by ADAA and published in The Journal of Clinical Psychiatry, Vol. 60, No. 7, July 1999. Accessed May, 2019.

[33]https://adaa.org/about-adaa/press-room/facts-statistics. Accessed April 5, 2019.

Chapter 7 – Downtime is NOT Wasted Time

[34]Ryan, John K. (1960) *The Confessions of St. Augustine: Translated, with an Introduction and Notes*. New York: Doubleday, p43.

[35]Paul, Marilyn. (2017) *An Oasis in Time: How a Day of Rest Can Save Your Life*. Emmaus, PA: Rodale Books.

[36]Berry, Wendell. (1987) *"1979, II" in Sabbaths*. San Francisco: North Point Press, p8.

Chapter 8 – Walk, Hike, Bike, Breathe

[37]Byrne, A., & Byrne, D. G. (1993). *The effect of exercise on depression, anxiety, and other mood states: a review*. Journal of Psychosomatic Research, pp565-574.

Chapter 9 – Tree Forts & Piles of Snow

[38]Louv, Richard. (2008) *Last Child in the Woods: Saving our Children from Nature-Deficit Disorder*. Chapel Hill: Algonquin Books, p36.

[39]https://stateofobesity.org/physical-inactivity/.   Accessed February 15, 2019.

[40]https://e360.yale.edu/digest/u-s-study-shows-widening-disconnect-with-nature-and-potential-solutions. Accessed February 15, 2019.

[42]Louv, p35.

[42]https://www.psychiatryadvisor.com/mood-disorders/nature-cognitive-anxiety-depression-mood/article/448018/.   Accessed February 23, 2019.

[43]Louv, p47.

[44]Louv, p109.

Chapter 10 – You Are What You Eat

[45]Byrd-Bredbenner C, Moe G, Berning J, Kelley D. (2019) *Wardlaw's Perspectives in Nutrition.* 11th edition. New York: McGraw-Hill Education.

[46]*Dietary Guidelines 2015-2020 Executive Summary.* https://health.gov/dietaryguidelines/2015/guidelines/executive-summary/. Accessed May 19, 2019

[47]*Choose My Plate.* https://choosemyplate.gov. Accessed May 19, 2019

[48]*MyPlate Plan:* 2200 calories, age 14+. https://www.choosemyplate.gov/MyPlatePlan_2200cals_Age14plus. Accessed May 19, 2019

[49]*What's Cooking? USDA Mixing Bowl.* https://whatscooking.fns.usda.gov. Accessed May 19, 2019

Chapter 11 – Creativity is NOT a Luxury

[50]Genesis 1:1 NKJV

[51]*All-Party Parliamentary Group on Arts, Health and Wellbeing Inquiry Report Creative Health: The Arts for Health and Wellbeing.* July 2017 Second Edition. Accessed April 5, 2019.

[52]*Adobe State of Create Study* 2012. Accessed April 5, 2019

[53]*World Economic Forum Report: The Future of Jobs.* Accessed April 18, 2019.

[54]L'Engle, Madeleine. (2001) *Walking on Water, Reflections on Faith and Art.* New York: Crown Publishing Group.

[55]Veith, Gene. (1991) *State of the Arts, From Bezalel to Mapplethrope.* Wheaton: Crossway Books.

[57]Dick Staub states, "The numbers of hours we spend listening to music, watching videos (TV, Netflix, Youtube) or engaging with any form of media is one of the loudest inputs into our lives." Dick Staub. (2007) *The Culturally Savvy Christian*. San Francisco, CA: John Wiley & Sons Inc., p12.

[57]Jantz, Gregory L. (2012) *Hooked: The Pitfalls of Media, Technology and Social Networking*. Lake Mary, FL: Siloam-Charisma House, p1.

[58]Media meets you right where you are to provide guidance and direction in a time when you desperately want and need both. It teaches you what to think, how to think, and how to live.

[59]Tolkien, J. R. R., and Douglas A. Anderson. (1994) *Letter to Editor, The Lord of the Rings*. Boston, MA: Houghton Mifflin Co., xii.

[60]Jantz, p2.

[61]The term translated "heart" refers to the human heart nearly 1000 times in both the Old Testament (814) and New Testament (159). It is probably fair to say that the heart features more than any other piece of the human anatomy.

[62]See also Ephesians 4:15-17, "Look carefully then how you walk, not as unwise but as wise, making the best use of time, because the days are evil. Therefore, do not be foolish, but understand what the Lord's will is."

[63]For a thought-provoking video displaying this, click https://www.youtube.com/watch?v=OINa46HeWg8.

[64] Wiersbe, Warren. (1993) *On Being a Servant of God*. Nashville, TN: Thomas Nelson, p3.

Chapter 13 – No Time!

[65]https://medium.com/carl-pullein/how-to-be-stoical-with-your-time-management-cc400630146b. Accessed May 10, 2019.

[66]https://www.purdueglobal.edu/blog/student-life/time-management-busy-college-students/ April 19, 2018. Purdue University Global. Accessed May 10, 2019.

Chapter 14 – Moving Forward

[67]https://www.entrepreneur.com/article/287870 By Nina Zipkin, February 2, 2017. Accessed May 28, 2019.

[68]https://www.aiuniv.edu/degrees/business/articles/smart-goals-for-college-students. Accessed May 28, 2019.

[69]Luke 13:31-33 New International Version

[70]https://stats.nba.com/leaders/?Season=2018 19&SeasonType=Regular%20Season. Accessed May 28, 2019.

[71]https://www.entrepreneur.com/article/287870. Article by Nina Zipkin, February 2, 2017. Accessed May 28, 2019.

Chapter 16 – Of Boats & Best Intentions

[72]Weaver, Harriett E. (1973) *Frosty: A Raccoon to Remember.* New York: Pocket Books.

[73]https://www.5lovelanguages.com/2018/06/the-five-love-languages-defined/. Accessed May 13, 2019.

[74]Rima, Samuel D. (2000) *Leading from the Inside Out: The Art of Self-Leadership.* Ada, MI: Baker Books, pp63-69.

[75]https://www.gallupstrengthscenter.com/. Accessed April 23, 2019.

Chapter 17 – Better Bank Accounts

[76]https://www.psychologytoday.com/us/blog/the-power-prime/201205/personal-growth-your-values-your-life. Accessed March 2019.

[77]https://www.cnbc.com/2018/06/26/money-is-more-stressful-than-work-or-relationships.html. Accessed March 2019.

[78]https://partners4prosperity.com/money-and-happiness-research/. Accessed March 2019.

[79]https://www.sparefoot.com/self-storage/news/1432-self-storage-industry-statistics/. Accessed March 2019.

[80]https://www.dictionary.com/browse/stewardship. Accessed March 2019.

[81]https://americasavesweek.org/research-shows-60-of-americans-are-spending-all-or-more-than-their-income/. Accessed March 2019.

[82]https://www.usatoday.com/story/money/personalfinance/20 17/11/18/a-foolish-take-heres-how-much-debt-the-average-us-household-owes/107651700/. Accessed March 2019.

[83]https://www.forbes.com/sites/zackfriedman/2019/02/25/student-loan-debt-statistics-2019/#21984ab5133f. Accessed March 2019.

[84]https://www.bankrate.com/finance/smart-spending/money-pulse-0115.aspx. Accessed March 2019.

[85]https://www.cnbc.com/2018/09/27/heres-how-much-money-americans-have-in-savings-at-every-income-level.html. Accessed March 2019.

[86]https://www.sciencedaily.com/releases/2017/07/170711112 441.htm. Accessed March 2019.

Chapter 19 – Stress

[87]Parts of this paper come from this review by Godoy LD, Rossignoli MT, Delfino-Pereira P, Garcia-Cairasco N and Umeoka EHL (2018) *A Comprehensive Overview on Stress Neurobiology: Basic Concepts and Clinical Implications.*

[88]Ibid.

[89]https://medlineplus.gov/ency/article/001942.htm. Accessed May 28, 2019.

Chapter 20 – The Giants of Anxiety & Depression

[90]https://www.apa.org/topics/stress/ Accessed May 31, 2019.

[91]American Psychiatric Association: *Diagnostic and Statistical Manual of Mental Disorders* – Fifth Edition (2013). Arlington, VA: American Psychiatric Association.

[92]https://www.nimh.nih.gov/health/statistics/mental-illness.shtml. Accessed May 31, 2019.

[93]Ibid.

Chapter 21 – When Just a Friend Won't Do

[94]https://www.counseling.org/about-us/about-aca/20-20-a-vision-for-the-future-of-counseling/consensus-definition-of-counseling. Accessed May 15, 2019.

[95]https://www.nami.org/NAMI/media/NAMI-Media/Infographics/Children-MH-Facts-NAMI.pdf Accessed May 15, 2019.

[96]Wang, P., Berglund, P., & Olfson, M. (2005) *Failure and delay in initial treatment contact after first onset of mental disorders in the National Comorbidity Survey Replication.* Archives of General Psychiatry, 62(6), 603-613.

[97]https://www.nami.org/NAMI/media/NAMI-Media/Infographics/Children-MH-Facts-NAMI.pdf   Accessed May 15, 2019.

Chapter 22 – Any Second Now

[98]Lucado, Max. (1991) *In The Eye Of The Storm: A Day in the Life of Jesus*. Dallas, TX: Word Publishing, pp108-111.

Chapter 23 – Don't Get Burned...Out

[99]Maslach, Christina. (2003*)   Burnout: The Cost of Caring*.   Los Altos, CA: Malor Book.

[100]Hart, Archibald D. (2007) *Thrilled to Death – How the Endless Pursuit of Pleasure is Leaving Us Numb*.   Nashville, TN: Thomas Nelson, Inc.

[101]http://www.churchlink.com.au/churchlink/forum/r_croucher /stress_burnout.html. Accessed March 6, 2019.

Chapter 24 – Becoming a (Self) Care-Giver

[102]National Association of Social Workers. (2018) *Professional self-care and social work*. In Social work speaks: National Association of Social Workers policy statements 2018–2010 (11th ed., pp257–264). Washington, DC: NASW Press.

[103]Hotchkiss, J. T. (2018) *Mindful Self-Care and Secondary Traumatic Stress Mediate a Relationship Between Compassion Satisfaction and Burnout Risk Among Hospice Care Professionals*. The American Journal of Hospice & Palliative Care, 35(8), 1099–1108. https://doi.org/10.1177/1049909118756657.   Accessed May 10, 2019.

[104]Aalbers, G., McNally, R. J., Heeren, A., de Wit, S., & Fried, E. I. (2018) *Social Media and Depression Symptoms: A Network Perspective*. Journal of Experimental Psychology: General. Advance online publication. http://dx.doi.org/10.1037/xge0000528. Accessed May 10, 2019.

Chapter 25 – I'll Be There For You

[105]Genesis 2:18 NIV

[106]https://jech.bmj.com/content/jech/59/7/574.full.pdf.   Giles, L. C., Glonek, G. F., Luszcz, M. A., & Andrews, G. R. (2005) *Effect of*

social networks on 10 year survival in very old Australians: The Australian longitudinal study of aging. Journal of Epidemiology & Community Health, 59(7), 574-579. Accessed May 2, 2019

[107]https://news.harvard.edu/gazette/story/2017/04/over-nearly-80-years-harvard-study-has-been-showing-how-to-live-a-healthy-and-happy-life/ . Accessed May 2, 2019.

[108]For your reading pleasure, the situations described in this chapter were taken from the following Scriptures: Matthew 28:16-20, Mark 2:13-17, Luke 14:1, Luke 5, Matthew 17:1–8, Mark 9:2–8, Luke 9:28–36, John 11:1-44, John 13:1-17, John 3:16, Matthew 26:36-46, Luke 22:39-46, Mark 14:32-42, Matthew 28:16-20.

[109]Identify "Safe Others" Scriptures: Ephesians 4:15, Galatians 5:22-23, Philippians 4:8, Romans 12:10, Matthew 5:37, Ephesians 4:15.

Chapter 26 – From Isolation to Community

[110]Collins, Jim. (2001) *Good to Great: Why Some Companies Make the Leap and Others Don't.* New York: HarperCollins, Publishers, Inc.

[111]Bonhoeffer, Dietrich. (1954) *Life Together: A Discussion of Christian Fellowship.* New York: Harper & Row Publications, p30.

Chapter 27 – Sharing the Journey

[112]https://www.imdb.com/title/tt0903624/plotsummary. Accessed April 1, 2019.

[113]https://www.merriam-webster.com/dictionary/mentor. Accessed April 1, 2019.

Chapter 28 – Get Over Yourself

[114]https://www.desiringgod.org/articles/deny-yourself-for-more-delight. Accessed May 15, 2019.

[115]See the Gospel of Mark 12:30-31

[116]https://www.huffpost.com/entry/volunteering7-reasons-why_n_6302770. Accessed May 17, 2019.

[117]http://www.league91.com/college-student-volunteering. *Seven Reasons You Should Not Volunteer as a College Student.* Accessed May 15, 2019.

[118]Ibid.

Chapter 29 – Surprised By Joy

[119]https://www.merriam-webster.com/dictionary/joy. Accessed May 13, 2019.

[120]https://gibbshappinessindex.com/blog/spirituality-and-happiness/ Accessed May 13, 2019.

[121]https://www.livescience.com/9090-religion-people-happier-hint-god.html. Accessed May 13, 2019.

[122]https://cslewisquotes.tumblr.com/post/42858497066/while-friendship-has-been-by-far-the-chief-source. Accessed May 13, 2019.

[123]https://www.berkeleywellbeing.com/well-being-survey.html. Accessed May 13, 2019.

Chapter 30 – An Attitude of Gratitude

[124]Emmons, R. A. (2013). *Gratitude works! A twenty-one-day program for creating emotional prosperity.* San Francisco, CA: Jossey-Bass, p24.

[125]https://www.ncbi.nlm.nih.gov/pmc/articles/PMC3489271. Hill PL, Allemand M, Roberts BW. *Examining the pathways between gratitude and self-rated physical health across adulthood. Personality and Individual Differences.* 2013; 54: 92-96. Accessed May 13, 2019.

[126]https://health.ucdavis.edu/welcome/features/2015-2016/11/20151125_gratitude.html. Emmons, R. A. *Gratitude Is Good Medicine.* Accessed May 2, 2019.

[127]2 Corinthians 5:21, Ephesians 2:4-8.

[128]John 14:16, Ephesians 4:12, Colossians 1:9-10, Hebrews 13:20-21.

[129]Romans 8:38-39.

[130]https://www.goodreads.com/quotes/267482-the-longer-i-live-the-more-i-realize-the-impact. Accessed May 23, 2019.

Chapter 31 – Lighten Up!

[131]A term that originated in popular NBC television show Parks and Recreation, when Tom and Donna two financially self-destructive adults that work in the Parks and Rec. Department of Pawnee, Indiana decide to spend an entire day pampering and spoiling themselves. However in the process end up destroying their bank accounts.https://www.urbandictionary.com/define.php?term=treat%20yo%20self. Accessed May 7, 2019.

[132]https://www2.ca.uky.edu/hes/fcs/factshts/hsw-caw-807.pdf. Accessed May 7, 2019.

[133]https://www.forbes.com/sites/daviddisalvo/2017/06/05/six-science-based-reasons-why-laughter-is-the-best-medicine/#3f2c667e7f04. Accessed May 7, 2019.

[134] https://www.forbes.com/sites/daviddisalvo/2017/06/05/six-science-based-reasons-why-laughter-is-the-best-medicine/#7ed235ab7f04. Accessed May 7, 2019.

[135] https://www.helpguide.org/articles/mental-health/laughter-is-the-best-medicine.htm/. Accessed May 7, 2019.

[136]https://www.rd.com/culture/laughter-facts/. Accessed May 7, 2019.

[137]From a 15 year study in Norway on the link between sense of humor and mortality. The study was conducted on over 53,500 people and found a 48% lower risk of death from all causes for women. Men had a 74% lower risk of death from infection. See the results at https://www.scientificamerican.com/article/laugh-lots-live-longer/. Accessed May 8, 2019.

[138]https://www.npr.org/sections/ed/2014/08/06/336360521/play-doesnt-end-with-childhood-why-adults-need-recess-too Accessed May 8, 2019. And here's the link to the National Institute for Play, www.nifplay.org.

Made in the
USA
Middletown, DE